"*CurbChek* chronicles the experiences of a Police Officer as he transitions from a new boot with challenging life experiences to a salty veteran who has been baptized into the dark side of reality by countless hours on the street.

"Follow along as the writer lives the terror and small triumphs that every cop has to face, not only through the course of a career, but also through each and every shift. We could all relate to each scene, contact, and scenario that he faced in the book. If you are reading this as a Police Officer, you will find your head nodding along in agreement with the thoughts and place yourself in each situation, as you have been there yourself."

• Justin, Website Administrator of
www.officerresource.com & Police Officer •

"I've told EVERYONE I know to buy it! I was getting a little lazy. Your book reminded me that people see the uniform, not the patch on the shoulder. You reminded me to be careful; thanks for that. I'll be first in line to buy your next book."

• D. Garcia •

"Your book was awesome. The way it was written was real. You told it how it was, and it should make people realize what cops have to go through."

• Ryan Waters •

"A gritty, fascinating read, and I recommend it to anyone."
• www.katesreads.com •

"Exciting, scary, sad, and sometimes darn right funny."
• www.allbooksreviewint.com •

CURBCHEK

ZACH FORTIER

steeleshark
press

Cover design, interior book design
and eBook design
by Blue Harvest Creative
www.blueharvestcreative.com

CURBCHEK

Published by
SteeleShark Press

ISBN-13: 978-0615816128
ISBN-10: 0-615-81612-6

Visit the author at:
Website: *www.curbchek.com*
Blog: *www.authorzachfortier.blogspot.com*
Facebook: *www.facebook.com/authorzach.fortier*
Twitter: *www.twitter.com/zachfortier1*
Goodreads: *www.goodreads.com/author/show/5164780.Zach_Fortier*

ALSO BY ZACH FORTIER

STREET CREDS

CURBCHEK-RELOAD

HERO TO ZERO

Preface

THE REALITY IS THAT ANY good street cop, the guy you praise and pin medals on, is damaged—really damaged.

The shit you see, it's battlefield intensity, urban warfare. Make no mistake about it: every cop who works the street—really works the street—knows this fact. Once you cross over into this twisted way of being, social niceties and folkways seem really stupid and pointless; it feels as if the façade the rest of the world lives with and accepts is shattered forever. You realize that the difference between the feeling of safety most people have in their day-to-day lives and the reality of the real world is only one thing: perception.

Your perception has changed permanently, and in any scenario violence and the breakdown of the façade are moments away. The reality is that the façade is incredibly thin, but we choose to live in it.

CurbChek

"Placing an unconscious or immobile individual's head against a curb with their mouth open, then stomping on or kicking them in the head."

"When a driver inadvertently hits or runs into a curb."

1 Is There A Problem, Officer?

THE POPULATION IS UP TO three-quarter million, but it's still a place where it's fairly easy to spot something out of place.

I was the south car that night, having returned to my old hometown—where I never intended to return.

I wonder how the taxpayers might feel if they knew that only three cars patrolled the entire unincorporated area of the county, all that space between the city and towns, the wide open patches between the islands of civilization. That's three cars and a sergeant, and maybe a K-9 unit—if we're lucky.

I was conducting extra patrols that homeowners or businesses had requested.

Most guys pencil-whipped this shit, but I was a little more obsessive about it. Seemed like we should check them; if there ever were a problem, I would've regretted not checking.

I checked this shopping unit complex every day I worked the south side. It was a photo supply business near the mouth of the canyon, and it was reporting break-ins. Nothing had ever been there before—but then one night I found a truck parked back behind the complex.

It was hidden, so the driver had to be trying to shield it from anyone's view on the street.

Tucked back in behind the building and in some trees, it gave me the creeps.

I backed out and re-approached, checking the area for snipers; there were none, of course. (I'd just come from a military background, and that was still fresh in my mind.)

I ran the license plates and checked them against the VIN; it all matched. I ran the car through NCIC, and it wasn't stolen. I checked the entire complex, and none of the businesses had been broken into.

This was weird shit.

The vehicle was parked that way for a reason; I just couldn't figure out why.

I had dispatch print the plate and cross-reference the registered owner with warrants, NCIC, and driver's license; nothing came up. I asked them to print it all out. I kept records of my own at the time to learn from, go back over, and see what I'd missed.

This was the part of police work that I'd always love: the small window of independence.

The military was good for training in tactics, firearms, marksmanship, and the extreme fitness that I still maintain today; however, there was no room for independent thinking or questioning anything. You did what you were told—always. You were never in charge; instead, you always waited for some rear echelon motherfucker—we called them REMFs'—to make a decision.

Move before you were told and you paid dearly.

Rank structure was severely ingrained in me.

Anyone who outranked you was in charge—which was just the opposite of real police work; on the street, the call was yours and yours alone.

At first, that was hard for me to get used to. A sergeant would show up, and the military training would kick in and I'd subordinate immediately.

Once I realized I could take the call and run with it, that it wasn't a test to see if I were insubordinate—I was all over it. I loved taking the call.

I respected no one's position in life based on his or her job or money, and I wasn't intimidated by much, so I'd listen to both sides and make my decisions.

Anyway, that night I was puzzled. What in the hell was going on?

I went to dispatch to pick up the printouts, and as I was leaving one of the dispatchers said she just got a call from a lady who wanted a friend of hers checked on.

She said the woman claimed that her friend's ex-husband had been calling her from Wyoming and making threats. The ex was a paranoid schizophrenic, and he sounded like he was off his meds. Her friend had called, and when she answered the phone it was dead. When she called back, there was no answer.

The last name matched the owner of the truck I'd just checked on—and the truck was from Wyoming.

I felt like an ass.

There I was, sitting there fumbling around with this truck; meanwhile, this guy was out there.

I hauled ass down to this missing woman's mobile home, which was near the mouth of the canyon where I'd come upon the parked truck that was so carefully hidden.

The door of the mobile home had been kicked in, so I called for backup and went in, clearing room-by-room, my gun out, searching.

I checked the entire trailer—which smelled like a damn litter box—and in the only bedroom I found an unmade bed covered in blood.

There was no one in the house.

I called for techs to process the scene and put out an attempt-to-locate on the woman's car; it was gone—and she with it.

I was pissed off.

I drove around the immediate area, looking for her car; then, call it intuition or whatever, I decided to park back up on a hill and blacked out (turned out my headlights).

I just sat, waiting.

I know this sounds weird, but I knew something was going to happen. Call it luck or gut instinct—whatever you want to call it to feel comfortable—but I knew I had to park and wait...something was coming.

Fifteen minutes later, her car came down the dugway.

I had one light out on my patrol car—which, as it turns out, was excellent strategy and perhaps should be taught at the academy.

I called in the car and began to follow until backup arrived. When backup showed up, I pulled the car over.

We lit it up big time and exited fast with two spotlights, both high beams, and take down lights pointed at the car.

I could see that there were two people, a male driving and a female passenger in the front seat—covered in blood.

She kept looking back, scared and bleeding; she looked like hell, but she was alive.

I walked to the driver, my gun out and pointed right at his head.

He said to me, "Is there a problem, officer?"

No shit, fuckhead. The woman bleeding next to you is not normal.

Thinking that this fucker was going to blow her brains out before I got there and get her away from him, I was wound-up, nervous, and edgy.

I told him, "Look at the barrel of my gun."

He did.

I said, "If you take your eyes off of it, move even a little bit, I will blow your fucking brains out. Do you understand?"

He said, "Yes, sir—but what's the problem?"

Seriously, he actually said it again.

Phil, my backup, had walked up to the other side of the car.

He asked, "Have you got him?"

I said, "Ya."

He said, "I'm gonna get her out of there. Be careful; shoot him if he moves."

We got her out, and I arrested the guy.

I was scared shitless, afraid I'd make a mistake and he'd get over on me and kill her before we could get her out.

I had been on the department about a year then, and I had very little experience with this kind of thing.

She said he'd told her that he was taking her out to kill her. He'd driven past the mobile home while we were processing the scene and was afraid because we were on to him so fast. When I dropped down the hill behind him with one light out, he relaxed.

She said she remembered his comment: "Cops never have a head-light out."

So he kept driving, calmly looking for a place to pull over somewhere near his truck and kill her, then walk back to his truck.

He'd broken into her home, pistol-whipped her, and dragged her by her hair out to her car to kill her.

I later found out that she was a teacher at one of the elementary schools nearby. She also knew my mother-in-law at the time...weird to see how she lived, and then taught kids? It blew my mind there was cat shit and garbage everywhere inside the trailer, and the filth was incredible.

This was my first real hard ass case; not the usual bullshit domestics, not running radar—but what I thought was real police work.

It was also what I saw as my first failure.

I felt that way because I was new and stupid, she'd nearly been killed.

I was very idealistic then, feeling I could make a difference—which, as it turns out, is a very stupid idea.

Anyway, after all that, a judge gave him probation because he'd gone off his meds and was mentally ill.

His breaking into her home, beating her up, and then taking her out to kill her in his state of mind supposedly didn't establish any intent to kill.

He was sent back to Wyoming and asked not to return. The judge made him promise to stay on his meds, and he was free to go. I was amazed that he wasn't forced into a grueling "pinky swear" marathon.

The next day at work, I found out that in police work if you do something well, the reaction from co-workers can be bizarre; some people hate you, and others envy you.

The sergeants I worked for were suddenly jealous of me, threatened by me—making me feel like I was isolated.

Other cops asked the lamest, most ass-backward questions.

"What was that like, kind of a rush?"

For me to get my thrills, I'd prefer that a woman isn't getting her head smashed in and living or dying based on my gut feelings.

I was at a loss; I had no idea what to think.

Later, when I went to the city force, I found out that prosecutors and the city cops all felt that the sheriff's office was a joke.

I could relate with that; I really didn't fit in there.

I felt like I needed to develop my skills, and if you worked at the county, the frequency of contact with real hardcore criminals was infrequent.

So, after a while I started to look seriously at the city police force; I felt it would be a better fit, giving me what I felt I was missing—but I was wrong...

2 Inside And Outside Reality

TWO WEEKS AFTER THE MARINE Barracks bombing in Lebanon in 1983, I was sent to Saudi Arabia as part of the military response deployed to stabilize the region.

You'd think that military training would translate into police work, just as I mistakenly thought when I found myself returning to my hometown years later; my best laid plans, though, quickly turned to shit.

Even back then, I was a cop, military police.

I knew that with my personality and various triggers, it was better for everyone concerned that I be something of an authority figure rather than be subject to authority figures without recourse.

In 1983, we waited in bunkers for suicide bombers from Iran to try to take out the AWACS stationed in Riyadh.

It was the easiest duty I ever had in the military; basically, I was there to keep the AWACS safe while the war was in session.

I'd dropped into a war zone from our Strategic Air Command (SAC) post. Coming from a base with nuclear capacity aircraft, I found Saudi a welcome relief.

We were given intelligence that said that small planes loaded with explosives flying under the radar were coming from Iran and to be prepared.

This was eighteen years before the 9/11 attacks on the World Trade Center and the Pentagon in 2001.

As soon as I got off the plane, the cops were separated from the rest of the military personnel. This was becoming a pattern: cops set apart from the rest of the population.

The hotel I was housed in was trenched, and cement barriers were in place all around it. There were machine gunners on the roof, but it was actually a break from SAC.

I slept like a baby, sat in bunkers all day in the heat, and drank a ton of water.

I watched the local vehicle traffic for any false moves, as well as constantly checking the skies for the prophesied Jihadist's small planes trying to kamikaze the AWACS; they never came.

I became friends with the Arab guards and learned some Arabic, broke bread, and ate lamb and rice.

I got along better with them than with some of the MPs who called them "sand niggers" and told me I was shit for befriending them. Fuck that!

I learned that they hated guys like Saddam and loved Jimmy Carter. They also thought that we Americans were arrogant pieces of shit.

After a while there, I couldn't help noticing some validity to their argument.

I agreed that you could pick out the Americans in a crowd, all loud, obnoxious, and foulmouthed; it was usually groups of kids one to three years out of high school, showing the world what America was all about.

Needless to say, there were times when I was embarrassed by the way my own people acted.

I had only one real brush with hostility while I was there.

One day, I went through the wrong gate and had an Arab guard hold a gun to my head.

He asked me if I was Islamic.

I said no.

He said I would die if I didn't swear to follow Allah.

I wasn't about to show any fear; I was—as I am now—stubborn (stupidly stubborn), so I refused and eventually told him to either get on with it and blow my brains out or let me through.

I warned him, though, that if he did shoot me he'd better start praying to Allah—because my MP brothers would torture him before they killed him.

We stared hard at each other, and he eventually decided to let me through.

Being stubborn—and a complete dumb ass—I couldn't let it end there, so I went back to my bunker and grabbed two cold drinks.

Then I drove back as fast as possible.

I was reckless—but obviously U.S. military with subdued decals on the vehicle.

I skidded to a halt, got out with M-16 in hand, and walked towards him with a purpose.

I stared at him hard for a second, then offered him one of the drinks as I cracked a smile.

He was shaking and scared, but he accepted my hospitality; he couldn't be sure I wasn't crazy.

Hardcore psychological warfare!

He'd been "Sacumsized!" a term we often used to describe the painful process of learning to survive in the command.

I was young and stupid, but he never messed with me again.

After that, I made a point out of going through his gate regularly; we even became friendly and on a first-name basis.

After about three months there, coming back to America was tough; having to go back to the grind of training, training, training—and then, just for a change, more training.

In the military, they try to break you with training.

We trained nonstop for a Russian nuclear attack, performing constant drills and training.

The planes would mock launch and roll down the runway, then stop and idle for a while, waiting for orders either to launch or return; eventually, they'd get their orders and turn around.

We trained for various scenarios, usually suicide attacks. We had a timed response to every possible penetration called a "15 in 5": we had to have a minimum of fifteen troops deployed in a minimum five minutes, ready and able to return fire at anything and everything.

Guarding the nukes, 15 in 5s, exercise after exercise, low-crawling in the dirt and then inspection the next day in the same boots, spit and polished—and they'd better be perfect.

After a few years, I worked my way into a Command and Control Center and watched one of these exercises from an observation tower.

One day while I was watching, it hit me: we were a suicide squad as well; constant drills lowered our ability to think about it, and our response was an immediate conditioned response, Pavlov dog style.

We trained to scan fields and buildings and watch traffic flows for anything out of the ordinary.

Seeing suspicious activity in nothing at all, paranoia became the norm, and having no real world threat or anything to gauge our imaginations against made us extremely neurotic.

Several guys had nervous breakdowns, and some would end up drinking heavily, fighting, and doing all kinds of stupid shit.

Looking back on it now, it was scary how an apparently normal guy could fall apart in a few short months under the stress. Some attempted suicide, and a few even succeeded. A lot went AWOL, showing up later in the correctional facility on base and doing hard labor.

We were the grunts of the Air Force; trained in army tactics, honed, and expected to be spit-polished, yet able to get down and dirty at the drop of a hat.

Some of us got good at it.

I buried myself in the combat competitions hosted by the SAC command. Doing this probably saved my bent head for a time.

Every SAC base sent a team to compete, and I was selected for our base's team and trained in combat tactics.

We practiced fighting teams of MPs in the field, studying and working out everyday.

The competition was away from the meat grinder of the nukes and the 15 in 5s; it was hard work, but a welcome break from the Nukes.

We won the Air Force obstacle course tournament as a team, and I set a course record my first year.

Suddenly, I was a celebrity—and I quickly learned that it wasn't a good thing and that people hated me for winning.

I ate dinner with generals, colonels, and the wing commander loved me and knew me by my first name. My uncle was a major and a B-52 pilot. The wing commander hated him, which made my uncle even more hostile toward me at my already fucked up family gatherings.

The police competition team of six cops from each base competed worldwide.

We were small tactical units defending nuclear weapons, aircraft, and the air bases. We practiced firearms training and overcoming larger groups of enemy teams with fields of fire and suppressive fire techniques.

It required extreme physical fitness and expert marksmanship and was considered a very elite competition, and our success got me the Saudi deployment.

We worked tactically, moving through fields and urban areas, looking for snipers, and conducting surveillance of areas you're assigned to protect.

SWAT training, building entry, aircraft and large vehicle recovery, becoming familiar—and even comfortable—with entering into dangerous situations, thinking and reacting based on training; essentially, what you'd learned and how you prepared mattered.

It required constant preparation, and after a while you could see the results. Those who didn't prepare or take it seriously were soon to fail—and fail hard; that, too, was a lesson.

Cops always have to be training and learning new things.

Being an MP in SAC also taught us to be respectful while remaining authoritative. It wasn't an easy task to respect a captain or a major who had violated some minor nuclear safety rule; to point the M-16 at their heads made it clear to them that you were respectful of their rank—but if they fucked up you'd most definitely kill them, or at the very least kick their ass.

Prima donna bitches that they were, the pilots hated this; they were coddled by everyone else but us, the MPs.

It was the recurring theme in my life: I was different even from the rest of the people who wore the uniform.

We were tasked with enforcing and protecting the nuclear arsenal from everyone, including the pilots who flew the planes loaded with the nukes themselves.

Set apart from the world, it was a familiar place to be, and it would continue to be throughout my career.

That was our mandate, our mission: to protect the nukes from everyone and anyone who might try to diminish the mission.

Everyone was suspect; no one was above the regulations.

Being an MP lacked opportunities for real experiences—besides training and drilling—that could transfer to civilian police work.

Independent thinking wasn't encouraged, and you were never in charge. Someone higher up always had to make the key decisions, and it seemed like there was no end to higher-ups. Rank was everything; on the "outside" (our term for the civilian world), the call is yours.

When I came in to police work on the outside, my military training was seen as a negative thing.

Cop tactics weren't military tactics; it was the late 80s, and the military was seen in a less than favorable light.

Tactics were seen as foolish and pointless, but as time passed they were seen as increasingly useful.

Moving as a small unit against an opponent requires fields of fire and trust in the guy next to you and behind you; you trust that they'll do their job, and you must do yours.

It teaches you to scan your surrounding environment, constantly searching for anything hostile. Just because you checked it once doesn't mean you shouldn't check it again—and then again.

You learned to handle your weapon in the dark, reloading, unloading, fixing failures by feel, not by sight, and we learned to shoot effectively at night before the invention of night sights.

Night shooting requires you to look off-center; the optical nerve is positioned in such a way that looking straight on at night makes it hard to see, and looking off-center enables you to see using your peripheral vision. I used that a lot in the inner city at night, walking in dark alleys in the never-sleeping city.

When I landed in the civilian cop world, the current idea on lighting when you entered a room or building was to flash the room and see what you could in a brief moment; the idea being that you didn't announce and excessively illuminate yourself, thereby making easy targets of yourself and others.

This was the cop theory at the time.

The reality, though, is that once you flash the room you've announced yourself quite well, and in the process destroyed your visual purple for at least another thirty minutes.

("Purple" being the moniker for the chemical that enables you to see at night.)

My thinking was to keep the light off until you needed it.

Once you turn it on, leave it on; you have at least 50-50 odds this way, and no one has the advantage—instead of being at a disadvantage, blind in the dark while your opponent can turn on his light to disorient you.

I was told, though, that this was a very stupid idea, and I was even ridiculed by my supervisors for arguing it.

I was being reckless and foolish with light according to the FBI, which is the cop source of validation in tactics and procedure.

Later—much later—the FBI came out and changed its opinion: keep the lights on.

I was no longer a reckless idiot, and the new theory was followed as mindlessly as the old one.

Homeless, Not Harmless 3

THE DARKER SIDE OF THE population, what lurks beneath, always fascinated me; like something reptilian and hungry that roils around in all of us, probing for openings and looking for a way out.

This was the layer under the day-to-day people (we called them "Daywalkers") who go to work, then go home and get to bed early enough to wake up in time to go to work again.

I'd begun stopping transients in the rail yards that bisected the county.

With plenty of "No Trespassing" signs, I had immediate probable cause. I would FI (field interview) and check them for warrants. If they had none, they went on their way...have a nice day.

If they had warrants, I arrested them and booked them into jail.

I found an amazing number of people on the run. It could be some really scary shit. Most of them have some serious mental illness; some are just trying to stay away from society.

Almost all of them, though, are armed—and some of them, I learned the hard way, are truly damn dangerous.

Transients hide troll-like under bridges and in every other place imaginable, pretty much anywhere there's heat or shelter or near the free medical or food services offered in every city.

They also campout, and there's a pecking order—with those who panhandle outside of liquor stores at the top.

Some put together fairly serious shelters, with even the occasional gas generator or corrugated metal sheets they scrounged for roofing. Some even take legit jobs at times.

I developed a series of locations that I'd hit and check for transients and their temporary camps. They really liked this old abandoned boxcar at the west end of the rail yards. It was parked near one of the free food kitchens, and the door opened away from the constant winds.

The railway workers never liked to mess with transients; they were too afraid of them. One of the bolder workers who confronted a transient who had crawled into an engine cabin had been stabbed.

One day I was looking in on that boxcar, and there were several guys inside of it, six or seven grown men. I checked them all and got to the last guy named Dan Campbell.

He was a big guy, about 6-foot-5, maybe 270 pounds—of which I am neither; he had me by at least 6 inches and 100 pounds.

He was talking shit to me, but he showed me his ID.

I ran him, and he was clean, no warrants.

I saw, though, that he had all these other IDs under different names and dates of birth, so I confronted him about it and asked him why he had so many—even though I already knew they used them to get food stamps in different states. They liked to trade the food stamps for cash, getting about fifty cents on the dollar, with which they could then buy booze.

Dan said just that, that he went from state to state and made more on food stamps than I made as "a Barney Fife here in this shit hole town."

I said, "Not anymore. Which one are you, really?"

He growled, "I'm all of them, but here I go by 'Dan Campbell.'"

"Well, Dan Campbell, here's your ID," I said. "I'm keeping the rest since they're all illegal IDs."

Pissed off now, he said, "You will give them back, or I'll kill you right here."

The fight was on.

He came at me, and I drew my nightstick and hit him in the chest, driving the point of the stick into him as hard I could; it didn't even slow him down.

I took two "home run" swings at his right knee, a knockout blow baton instructors promised would end any attack because the bad guy's knee would collapse; Dan's knee did *not*.

I threw the nightstick as far as I could so he couldn't use it against me, then I started to fight him hand-to-hand.

The guys he was with were cheering and rooting for him, yelling at him to kill me and talking shit to me about how they were going to take my gun and badge after he did.

I somehow managed to call for backup as we were wrestling, but no one knew how to get to where I was.

While we battled, police cars rolled back and forth and lights and sirens were going off.

There were city and county cars and lots of lights and noise—but not a lot of brains; no one could seem to find us.

After I pushed him against my car, I finally got one handcuff on his left wrist. I then kept him against the car, kidney punching him and trying to get his left arm back behind him.

When the sirens started getting closer, his supporters ran back to the boxcar as a group.

I thought they were getting the hell out of there, hoping not to get caught...I was wrong.

They went back to Dan's pack and got out a .22 caliber handgun that he kept there and loaded it. Then they looked out.

I was slowly wearing Campbell down; he was getting tired.

Suddenly, though, he reached back with his right hand and grabbed my holstered gun. I tried to break his grip but couldn't; he had it solid.

Two weeks before, I'd purchased a Safariland Level 2 retention holster from one of my few friends at the sheriff's office. He was a dealer in that kind of equipment, and I felt it would be a wise investment with all the interviews I was doing in the rail yards. This turned out to be a really good idea.

Campbell was aware that he had a hold of my gun and that I couldn't break his grip. He was too damn strong and big, so my only remaining advantage was endurance.

He pulled hard, trying to get my gun out of the holster and lifting me off the ground in the process, leaving both my feet dangling like a little kid. Fortunately, though, the holster held. Then, I got a burst of adrenaline, broke free, and started punching his kidneys as fast as I could, using both hands as I let his cuffed hand go. It was a gamble, but it worked.

He was really hurt at that point, so I pulled him to the ground by the hair and finally cuffed him.

Meanwhile, the group had started to depart the boxcar with the loaded gun and walked toward us, so I knelt on Dan's back, drew my gun, and faced his friends as they started towards me; they all stopped.

I heard one say, "Holy shit, he got the best of Dan!"

I started talking shit back to them.

"So which one of you transient fucks was gonna take my badge?"

They threw something in the boxcar, then ran off in different directions.

I was breathing hard, so I tried to rest up.

I radioed the patrol cars still driving around with lights and sirens going and directed them to the boxcar. I then arrested Campbell and recovered his gun—which was what his friends had thrown back into the boxcar—then booked him into jail.

Sometime during this period, I started to figure out that it wasn't "us against them" as I'd been led to believe.

When you're in the academy and new on the street, you're taught either directly or indirectly that it's us (cops) versus them (everyone who isn't a cop).

Campbell would be the first of many experiences that led me to realize that that mindset was wrong.

An hour after I booked his giant ass into jail, I was called back to do a medical transport. Guess who?

Campbell was complaining of chest pain from where I drove the stick into his chest, and his knee had swollen up huge.

He was blind drunk when we went toes and had felt nothing—but now I had to take this bruised shit bag to the hospital to be treated?

I was annoyed, but I had to do it; I was the south car, and that was one of my responsibilities.

On the way, he tried to apologize to me, saying he'd been drinking whiskey all night and that it made him crazy. He said that he meant no harm. His apology, taking him to the hospital, and dealing with the damage I'd inflicted during our battle made him seem human to me, and not just an enemy.

Having to see that he was beat to hell really hurt me, and sorrow truly struck me.

Of course, I never acknowledged that to him—or anyone else—but it bothered me that I believed him. I realized that we're all in this together.

People make huge mistakes in their lives. They have poor coping skills, act on impulse, and later regret what they've done. They get waking-up-on-the-lawn drunk and do things they'd normally never even consider. Their judgment goes out the window—and their lives with it.

Basically, the reality is as hard to handle as it is to accept: given the right set of circumstances, anyone is capable of anything.

So, from that point on, this incident with the homicidally-drunk and later apologetically-sober hulking rail rider changed how I talked to people, as well as how I treated them.

He was truly sorry—but that didn't change the fact he wanted me dead and had seriously tried to kill me.

He was later convicted and did a few months in jail. I never saw him again.

4 Huffing To Death

ONE DAY, I WAS DISPATCHED to a report by frantic parents and neighbors for a kid who had passed out in a garage on the north side. They had no idea what was wrong. He started screaming horribly after he regained consciousness.

He was only about ten or eleven years old and was told by a friend that sniffing starter fluid would make him really high.

He'd skipped school, and after his parents left for work he'd gone back into the garage and started to huff starter fluid.

Apparently, he'd done this enough times before that he needed to increase the amount in order to get the same effects.

This time he'd passed out, falling on the can—and landing on it in such a way that it continued to spray onto his face until it had emptied.

He awoke a while later and was immediately in considerable pain, at first uncomfortable but it quickly became unbearable.

He began to scream, and the neighbors heard him and called us.

I'd arrived before medical and backup, but none of us were able to help; no one had ever heard of something like this before.

When we arrived, his face had begun to swell; the starter fluid had caused a cold burn, damaging his facial tissue by freezing it, and as the flesh warmed up it began to swell.

He continued to scream loudly, but there wasn't much we could do except to try to calm a tortured and terrified little boy.

Emergency medical arrived and immediately called for a "life flight" helicopter to take him to a hospital burn unit that might have some experience with what we were watching.

His face continued to swell to the point where his eyelids squeezed shut, and his tongue and lips also swelled until they were rock hard. It got so bad, one eye orbit popped the gel inside—and the eyeball drained down his face. He just continued screaming in agony.

The helicopter landed, and the paramedics immediately loaded him up and flew off. He never made it to the hospital; he died en route, his lungs filling with fluid—which caused him to drown.

5 Move Along, Citizen

ANOTHER NIGHT WHILE PATROLLING, I came across a vehicle parked in the canyon.

I'd been checking the area thoroughly since residents had been calling in about a transient who'd made his way from the rail yards to the canyon and was living in the woods above their houses.

I stopped and got out to check on the small pickup truck. Maybe it was some drunk or possibly someone kicked out of his house by his wife, left with no choice but to sleep in the truck; instead, I found a guy who had on a satin blouse, bra, mini-skirt, and high heels.

As I approached, I saw that he wore makeup, had on earrings, and had pulled up the mini-skirt and pulled down his panties and pantyhose—and was masturbating to several magazines featuring naked men that were spread out around the inside of the truck.

I asked him, "What do you think you're doing?"

He jumped.

He hadn't heard me walk up; he was so engrossed, he had no idea I was there.

"Nothing," he said as he pulled up his underwear and readjusted his skirt.

I asked him for his license and registration, then checked him for warrants; he had none. His record may have been clean, but I still had questions.

I went back and talked to him, explaining that he had no warrants but that he wasn't free to go until we discussed what the hell he was doing in his truck alone in the dark, dressed up like a woman. I had to get a sense as to whether or not he was any kind of threat to the residents nearby.

He told me that he frequently dressed up and pretended to be female, and he said that he often came up into the canyon "to get in touch with his feminine side."

He said that he was married and that his wife didn't know about this behavior—and that he'd appreciate it if she didn't find out. I said that she wouldn't.

He wasn't gay, he said, just interested in cross-dressing because he felt that there was a woman inside him that occasionally needed to escape.

I said, "OK, but in the future let her escape somewhere else. I don't want to see you up here again—or your wife *will* find out. Deal?"

He agreed and left.

6 Learning The Hard Way

STILL VERY GREEN AND OUT to help the public, I was on patrol one night and spotted a driver going the wrong way on a one-way street at two in the morning. Foolishly, I thought he had to be lost, so I pulled the car over.

I was still developing my personal technique for traffic stops—and this one was about to change it drastically.

Immediately after I turned on the overheads, the driver pulled over and exited the vehicle. His passenger also got out.

The two men were both walking back to my patrol car with a purpose, almost running. They even made eye contact with me. They weren't acting like anyone I had ever pulled over before.

It was then that I realized that I'd made a huge mistake. Mentally, I was in the wrong place.

Intent on helping the poor citizen obviously lost and going the wrong way, I'd prematurely made up my mind about what was going on and how the stop would unfold—instead of just letting the situation define itself and being ready for whatever that would be.

In seconds, I was in real shit—and sorely unprepared: I was wearing a seat belt, the car door was closed, and I hadn't even come to a full stop yet.

I had to get the belt off, the door open, and get the car stopped immediately—or they'd be on me.

I barely accomplished all this in time to draw my weapon, yelling at the driver to get back to his car with my gun in his face.

In hindsight, that, too, was stupid. The gun was too close to him; he could have grabbed it—and then I would've been completely screwed.

I also hadn't kept an eye on his partner. Fortunately for me, though, they barely knew each other.

Somehow, I got out of my car in time to stand behind my car door, and I aimed my gun at the driver, yelling at him to get back into his vehicle. He decided to do what I told him, and so did the passenger.

I then called for backup, and fortunately my sergeant was only a few blocks away. When he rolled up, I started to dig into what the hell was going on.

It turned out that the driver was fresh out of prison; he'd been released for less than twenty-four hours, and he'd stolen the car and met the passenger in a bar. He wanted to buy some cocaine, and the passenger knew where he could get some. They were on their way to the dealer when I stopped them.

The passenger said that when I pulled them over, the guy told him he wasn't going back to prison and that he intended to get to my car and kill me before I could get out.

The passenger was afraid of him, so he went along with the plan out of fear.

I was lucky there was no real alliance, agreement, or understanding between them. The passenger was done with the plan the moment my gun came out, and he saw that any fight would be deadly for both of them. I really didn't have anything on the passenger, so I let him go and booked the driver into jail.

He was, of course, very pissed off, and he started talking shit and threatened that once he got out of prison he'd kill my entire family, torture my children, rape my wife, my dog, the neighbor's cat, blah, blah. All of it was added to the paperwork for his parole officer.

I never saw him again, but I also never wore my seatbelt again—even though it was required by department policy.

From then on, I always started my traffic stops from a greater distance, and I made sure that the car door was slightly ajar.

The thought of assisting the needy, harmless public was gone; in my mind, any stop that I made was for that same guy—with his same intent to kill me. This strategy would save my ass over and over again.

I'm aware of the fact that helping the wayward public is a nice idea, but the fact is, that's rarely the reality. Cops aren't firemen; we have to battle with people who don't want us to do the job that we're hired to do.

Another incident that made me stop and think was a call from a couple who answered a knock at their door to find a woman they didn't know. She just walked into their home, acting strangely, then locked herself into their bathroom and refused to come out.

I was patrolling a foothill part of the city at the south end of the county when the call came over that the woman had finally come out of the bathroom and left, taking the keys to the couple's truck.

The chase led all over the suburbs just to the south, and it soon came toward me. She was running stop signs and somehow hadn't hit anything.

I started out last in the long line of several cars chasing her. The acceleration contest then led up to the area known as "The Dugway," four lanes cut into the hillside for about five miles with a long drop over the south side if a motorist got through the guard rail.

She weaved across the oncoming lanes of traffic once or twice, almost touching the guardrail, and we thought she was going to launch.

Driving at speeds of over 100 mph, by the time she led us over the Dugway she was headed to the start of the main drag that spanned about fifteen miles northbound and led to the heart of the county—which was filled with some 180,000 people who were mostly sound asleep and had no idea that we were coming; all they heard were sirens in the night.

Eventually, I'd somehow become first in line and was rolling behind her at 120 miles an hour, running red lights as fast as my Crown Vic could go.

When I pulled up slightly behind her and to her right, she tried to hit me a few times. Gradually, I pulled up alongside her, and we made eye contact—and she promptly smiled, then tried to ram me again.

I pulled a little ahead of her and rolled down my window, then threw a large soft drink at her windshield, which caused a big spray of water.

The guys behind her yelled to each other over the radio that it wouldn't be long now; they thought she'd just blown a radiator hose. I threw the drink because I was pissed off that she'd tried to hit me; this was getting personal.

By then, other units had been able to form a safe corridor, blocking all the intersections ahead; so, we kept going.

We'd covered some ten miles in about four minutes when she suddenly cut east to turn onto the state highway that led up a canyon.

Not really a highway, it's just a road cut out between a river and a mountainside with no shoulders most of the way; just a single narrow lane in each direction.

She had an amazing control of the vehicle while she flew up the canyon at about sixty-five miles per hour, doubling the posted speed limit.

I was having trouble keeping up; she was somehow able to hold that speed, but I couldn't. I had to slow down while she power slid through the sharp corners into oncoming traffic lanes, somehow free from oncoming cars. All the way up the canyon we went, about nine miles total.

We drove past the dam at the top of the canyon, then started running alongside its reservoir.

At that point, another patrol car joined me, and we tried to box her in three times—but she'd always accelerate or weave at the right time.

Finally, though, she accelerated too much and rolled over, tumbling down into the reservoir.

We stopped and left our cars, running down through the brush to where the truck had gone into the water. We stopped at the water's edge, and I was thinking that I'd have to dive in and get her out when I suddenly heard splashing and coughing farther out in the water.

She'd been thrown clear of the now destroyed, totaled truck and was swimming back to shore—and she'd somehow come out of this rollover and 125 mile-an-hour chase with nothing more than minor scratches.

Later, we found out that she was so high on cocaine that she had no idea what she was doing.

Riverview PD had to clean up the mess because it was technically their case; we just wrote reports.

I couldn't help wondering *What the hell? Flying across the county through the city and up the canyon at these speeds because some woman was coked up?*

It seriously made me rethink chases, and I realized that I had to calm down and not get so drawn into the moment, instead looking at the bigger picture.

High-speed chases are always debated and probably always will be. You either endanger the citizens while chasing criminals or endanger the people if the criminals know you won't chase.

If either choice allows a suspect to hurt someone down the road, the department gets sued and attorneys pull your GPS to track every inch of every move you either made or chose not to make. Classic "Damned if you do, damned if you don't."

On-the-job training isn't just about the crazed ones who come right at you; it's also about those who look away.

I'd answered a call from a woman whose house was broken into in a town called Wolfstone. The burglar made himself at home, taking the time to eat and rifling through her underwear drawer.

It made for an unusual crime scene; it would've been more typical if a stereo or at least some silverware had been taken.

What the burglar had done had an intimate feel to it; he'd made a point to get as close to her sexually as he could. She no longer felt safe in her own home.

When I asked who she thought might have done this, she hesitated at first, then finally said her paperboy, a 14- or 15-year-old kid.

He gave her the creeps with the way he looked at her, and he was always hanging around. She thought she'd seen him outside one of her windows late at night, but he'd vanished when she got up to look.

I had her walk me through what had been taken or tampered with. The kid drank a two-liter bottle of Mountain Dew, ate some cookies, then opened her drawers and had gone through her underwear. She said that panties were missing and she described them, then she gave me his name and address.

I went to talk to the family, speaking to the parents and explaining what had happened and that the boy was a suspect.

I asked for permission to talk to him, and they agreed.

After about an hour in my car with me, the boy admitted to going into the home and drinking the soda and eating the cookies—but he wouldn't admit to taking the panties.

I then sat him down and talked to him and his parents together.

Crying and screaming, he denied it—but in the end it was obvious that he'd been in the house and through her drawers.

He left the room, and I talked to the parents, asking them to get him some help. This was a burglary; by definition it was a felony, but the complainant didn't want to press charges. She just wanted him to stop and get help.

I explained this to them, letting them know that if he didn't get help it was very possible that he'd escalate his behavior and move on to larger, worse crimes.

The parents exchanged a strange glance, then stared hard at each other for a few minutes.

The father then began to cry, and the mother said something about thinking that they were protected from this sort of thing.

She said, "We're Christians, devout churchgoers living the life the gospel requires. This isn't supposed to happen to us."

Their home was filled with paintings of Jesus and other religious imagery amid the sparse furniture. The father just sat there and cried quietly for a while, then they said that they'd get some help for their son and thanked me.

Something about that long stare that they shared bothered me; it seemed that there was a lot of nonverbal communication passing between them, so I started to dig.

I had a hard time getting any information at first, but eventually I found out that the dad had a record. He'd gone through the expungement process, though, and there wasn't much left. One department had a picture of him in an old file—but it was just a picture, nothing else.

Then I found out that the couple's other two sons had been arrested as juveniles for sexually abusing the neighborhood kids, raping and sodomizing the littlest ones.

Something about the dad still bothered me, though, but all I had was the picture, so I went around with it from police department to police department—then finally a veteran cop recognized him immediately.

He said the father had been a serial rapist from the late 60s and early 70s.

He'd raped several women on the east side of the city and was finally caught when he raped a little girl.

The old-timer said he was brutal and had made the comment that if he'd killed the little girl when he had the chance he never would've been caught; she was the only victim who could positively identify him.

I kept checking and found out that the guy had taught school after he'd been released from prison.

His record had been expunged after he'd been let go for molesting little kids in elementary schools. He hadn't been charged; just fired. I learned about this from talking to teachers and janitors at the schools; one story led to another, and then another.

I also found out that he'd met his wife through church.

She honestly believed that if they lived the life the church required, his evil ass nature would be cured. She also thought that as long as they paid their tithing, attended church regularly, said their prayers, and lived by the scriptures, everything would be fine.

She'd married a serial rapist, knowing exactly what he was; she was aware that he'd continued on to sexually abuse children as a teacher.

I'd guess he abused his own children as well. The statute of limitations had passed, but it was an eye-opener for me to see just how criminals hide out in plain sight.

Years later, I'd meet the kids.

When I spoke with them, it seriously freaked them out that I knew who they were. They were paranoid, openly upset, and they wanted to know how I knew them.

I just told them that I knew them from Wolfstone; there wasn't much to talk about after that. I was no longer a cop by then, but what I learned while I was talking to their parents that day made me much more aware of the nonverbal cues that people give out.

It's important to listen to what's not being said; usually, it's much more important than what *is* being said.

Another hard lesson learned came when I was still with the county but in one of the bigger cities.

There was a large auditorium in one of the civic centers and the managers were trying to it make profitable by renting it out. Normally, this wouldn't be our problem; we were county cops, and this was in the city. One night, however, one of our guys had been poaching in the city, trying to get drunken driving arrests.

He came upon a large riot in progress at the civic center as a large wedding in the auditorium had ended, spilling out onto the grounds. When he called for help, I responded.

The scene was a chaotic mess with people running everywhere, swinging bats, sticks, and chains, and one group was beating the hell out of a guy on the ground.

That's where the other deputy was when I arrived; he was trying to break up the group kicking the hell out of the guy.

I pulled up fast, high beams and overheads on, and hit the siren.

The group scattered, then the other deputy yelled at me to chase a specific guy—as he had a knife and had been stabbing the victim.

I was out of the car and running after him. He took off behind the building, and I was right behind him; once again, like a dumbass I was caught up in the chase.

The area was all rail yards and gravel, and we ran all across tracks and around boxcars. Finally he gave out, and I landed on top of him, cuffed him, and then caught my breath. I never found the knife.

For a few minutes, we just lay there, both of us breathing hard—then we heard his friends; the same ones who had been kicking the shit out of the guy on the ground were now looking for us. We were in the pitch dark, and they were trying to find him.

They were all around us, calling out to him. He yelled back once, then they started running around, frantically trying to locate where the sound came from.

"Let us know where you're at, Holmes" they said, "and we'll get you out of here!" I heard one guy say, "We'll fuck that cop up! He's alone... we'll get you out of here. Where are you?"

Then I heard, "Here piggy, piggy, piggy. We're gonna fuck you up, bitch!"

I grabbed my suspect by the throat and clamped down until he started to gag.

I then said to him in as violent a whisper as I could, "One fucking word, and I will crush your fucking throat. You will have an accident: you got hurt when you fell down. Understand, motherfucker?"

He managed to gasp, "Ya."

We lay there for a while, listening to his friends running around in the gravel, trying desperately to find him while calling to each other and making threats to me.

Finally, some city cops showed up and shined flashlights into the rail yards, looking for us; this scared off his friends.

When it was safe, we got up and walked back the deputy who'd sent me off on this little chase.

I was pretty proud of myself; I'd caught the guy and got off with no injuries. I walked over to the deputy and tried to give the bad guy over to him, as this was part of his case. He refused to take him, though.

I was confused. "What's up, man? You told me to chase him. He was supposed to have a knife, remember? You said he stabbed your guy?"

He looked me straight in the eye and said, "Well, I never saw any of that. I didn't think you'd be able to catch him, and I can't identify him from the group. Besides, I don't want to write a report on this. Just book him for intoxication, and let's go."

I couldn't believe this shit!

I was hot—*really* fucking hot. I checked, and the guy did have warrants, so I booked him on the warrants as well. The city cops wouldn't even look at him as a suspect. Their exact words were, "One Mexican stabbed another Mexican. Happens all the time! We don't fucking care. He's yours."

I did some more checking, and I found out that he was a gang member out of California hanging out with a local gang family in the city.

The whole night had been surreal. I'd done it again: got caught up in someone else's call, caught up in the moment and the emotion, and put myself in danger again for nothing.

My fellow deputy and I were no longer on speaking terms after that. He had the balls to tell everyone that I'd gone after the guy for no reason and didn't let anyone know where I was going. He also told them that I was careless and unsafe and to be careful around me.

I was learning.

7 SWAT—Sometimes It's Personal

YOU MAY BE SURPRISED TO hear that SWAT calls can actually be a time for thoughtful introspection, a time to think about things as we're getting paid to put on the gear, arm up, then park our asses and wait on an outcome.

After getting the call, we'd hustle in from whatever detail we were on. We tried to get to the scene fast enough to gear up while team commanders measured the actions required to end whatever cluster the patrol division had already cordoned off.

This gathering of pent-up officers, though, soon fell abruptly at ease for hours, which would give us down time for things to gel in our heads.

Often, I'd think about things like how damn strange it was coming back to my hometown as a police officer.

I never had any intention of coming back to this place; the site of my massively dysfunctional childhood was no place to reminisce.

I came back for my second wife—huge mistake.

We'd known each other in high school (not as well as I thought, it turned out) and kept in touch. When we got married, the real nightmare began.

My marriages tend to work out only when I pull night shifts, giving me more time with the kids while avoiding the wife...well, at least my first three marriages did.

Cops never seem to marry well, though, so at least we all had that in common to chat about.

"Love" isn't enough; there's something about the lurid demands of a job you can never explain to a spouse who just doesn't want to hear about it anyway.

"How was your day?"

"Shit up to my knees, and you?"

Then my first child was born, and there was no going back; making the city a better place suddenly became very important to me.

I also still had this feeling that I could make a difference with my military experience, having grown up in the city as well. I never really mentioned that to anyone until now, but it was always there in the back of my mind.

During the waiting time, the lulls on SWAT calls, I also had the chance to become amazed at my fellow officers' lack of any real connection with the people whose circumstances we'd surrounded; of course, most of them weren't deploying in their old childhood stomping grounds like I was every time we set up in the inner city. My fellow "ninja turtles" were often learning that fact about me for the first time.

I'd already kicked ass enough times, though, that I guess they knew it wouldn't be an issue. Nobody ever said anything about my roots. Of course, I never gave up much about my childhood. I didn't see it as much to tell.

To this day, I think I'm still owed a childhood and have got one coming, as mine wasn't childlike at all; it was more like a fifteen-round title bout. I'm much more edgy than most people—even more than most cops.

I think it was something that I developed even before I became a cop, likely from an upbringing of battling nonstop and having nowhere to turn to escape, no time to be a kid and just grow up naturally.

I went from a hostile home environment to a hostile school environment, and on the way to and from there were battles every day. Most kids might get into a fight once in a while, but not me.

My mother was quite literally a crazy woman; she pitted my brother and me against each other from the time we could walk.

We hated each other, a relationship that still grows richer in its span of distance to this day. He'd pick fights for me with the older kids, loving to antagonize them against me.

I'd be walking home, and they'd be waiting, older, bigger, and stronger. As a result, I learned how to handle myself—and fuck people up severely if I had to.

Most days, we'd pass the old Clark Market. It was where my brother liked to wait for me.

One day, I was in a fight again—and I was losing—hating, as I always did, the way I felt fighting.

I was still confused as to why I had to fight more than anyone else I knew—then survival kicked in, and I got out from under the older kid and really hurt him.

There was lots of blood in the snow around us, his and mine; I'd gone crazy.

Old man Clark came out and pulled me off—then I hit him, too, launching F-bombs everywhere as he threw me down and called me an animal.

I was the animal?

He said that I should leave the older kid—the bigger kid—alone; I was in the first grade, and he was in the fifth—and twice my size.

I jumped back on him, not wanting him to be able to fight me another time, then Old man Clark went after me again.

That was how I grew up. My parents either didn't care or were unaware of it—and looking back, I wonder why they had us at all.

So, I had this weird craving for peace, and at the same time I never wanted to be the subject of some cheese dick's authority over me.

Police work somehow made sense.

Standing around on SWAT calls led me too often to these thoughts and others. Often, more important for me was bracing for the occasion when I'd have to draw down on some fucked up bastard I'd known for years; the possibility was much more likely on SWAT calls.

SWAT comes in after the fact; there was no chance for me to be among the first on the scene, where I could talk to people and probe for some kind of connection, like an uncle or a cousin of the suspect's that I might know. When SWAT was called out, that point was long past for the most part.

So when I put on the camo, the helmet, the body armor, and took up the assault rifle, that was when I had to wonder if I might have to shoot someone that I'd sat next to in the third grade, or whose father I went to high school with, or maybe I dated his daughter or fought his brother in a schoolyard fight...the possible combinations were mind-numbing, and it was difficult to put them out of my head.

One day, a SWAT call became more personal for my teammates.

Finally, all at once, all my fellow officers would know what it was like to go out on a messy human entanglement where they had a personal, visceral connection; I'd get to stop wondering how these chumps couldn't see what it could do to your insides to roll up on some-one you knew.

It was the first time that I saw on their faces some kind of an emotional reaction to a call.

Suzanne Wilson was a dispatcher whom I'd known since I started working in law enforcement. She worked nights, as I did, and I became friends with her and others. We'd often talk about calls because dispatch-ers hardly ever hear about the outcomes after they send patrol cars and ambulances out cruising around the county.

They had all kinds of information at their fingertips, though, with access to multiple massive databases. So we'd talk about the job, kids, spouses, or whatever came up.

This SWAT page came for a little town on the west side of the county. While composed mainly of city officers, it was multi-jurisdic-tional, so we could end up anywhere.

This was a hostage situation; the caller had asked for help after her husband had gone ballistic, and several shots had been fired.

We were staging in the basement of a home down the street.

The entire team showed up, about sixteen guys total, but the situation dragged on for a while. Snipers were out on the perimeter, and it was a brutally cold night.

Negotiators were working with the guy inside the house, trying to keep a conversation going. Initially, he wouldn't say what had happened; just that he wanted out of the relationship with his wife. She and her oldest daughter had confronted him, accusing him of having an affair. They all got into an argument, and when he felt that his wife was trying to destroy his life, he just lost it.

As it turned out, this was Suzanne's husband.

It took a while for us to put together the fact that this was the same Suzanne Wilson, emergency dispatcher.

Suddenly, it was all very personal.

This wasn't some random family of strangers nobody knew; I'd talked to her for hours, shared our personal lives, and laughed over the same things.

Suzanne was in the house, and we didn't know if she was dead or alive; all we knew for sure was that we had contact with her husband and he wouldn't let the women come to the phone.

We waited while the negotiators did their thing, ready to go into the house at a moment's notice.

Eventually, they got Mr. Wilson talking, and he opened up and admitted to shooting Suzanne and her daughter. He didn't know if they were dead or not. He came out peaceably and surrendered to us, then we went in and cleared the house.

Suzanne and her daughter were both dead and had been for hours. It was a hollow feeling, alternately filled with pangs of helplessness, then rage.

It would turn out that the folks of any substance I knew before had gotten out of the inner city, and the time would come when I'd put a bullet in someone I knew—blowing holes in my childhood.

Das Boot 8

ALZHEIMER'S AND THE DEVIL MAKE for one terrified old woman, I'd discover one night as I was dispatched to an unknown call, a possible burglary in progress.

An elderly lady had reported someone prowling around outside of her house. She said that she was alone and afraid, and could we please hurry.

When I arrived and got out of the car, I heard this incredible screaming—but it wasn't just any screaming; it was unlike anything I've heard before... an agonizing, blood-curdling, continuous cry of pure anguish like someone was getting viciously tortured inside the house.

There was no time to wait for backup; just time enough to describe the situation to dispatch and tell them that I was going in. I asked them to start medical rolling.

I stood at the door, gun drawn, and yelled, "Police! Open the door!"

More horrific screams came, then an eerie silence as I heard footsteps approaching the door from the other side.

A deep, guttural male voice said, "Go away," then I heard more footsteps away from the door—and the screams started again.

I leaned back and kicked the door in, and it slammed against something small and white, sending it skidding under a table.

I cleared the house, going from room to room and yelling, "Police! Show me your hands!" looking for the suspect in what I was sure would be a horrific scene.

No one was there, though, so I continued to yell out, "Let me see your hands!"

It was a bluff; I couldn't find anyone.

Then I heard something behind me; a rustling of some kind back in the living room where I entered the home.

Completely mystified, I entered the room and noticed movement under the table. I decided to challenge whoever was underneath. "Come out, hands first! Slowly..."

Two small, frail, aged and bloodied hands came shaking out from under the table, skin torn on the forearms; it was a small, terrified elderly woman, shaking and timid. I helped her up and asked what happened.

To make a long story short, she had both Alzheimer's and a devout religious faith. She was the only one in the house and had called because she was frightened; she was sure the devil was prowling outside, trying to get in to take her away—and I'd unwittingly fulfilled that prophecy with my pounding at her door.

She said she came to the door and made her voice as deep and menacing as possible, hoping to scare me—"the devil"—away.

Then, when I kicked the door in, she was still behind it—and was knocked across the room and under the table, scraping the skin on her arms. Other than that, she wasn't injured.

Embarrassed beyond belief, I canceled back up and waited.

Dee, the dispatcher on the call whom I knew really well, kept checking on me and couldn't understand what had happened—and I wasn't about to tell her. She had a wicked sense of humor, and I wasn't ready to be humiliated. I still had a small glimmer of hope that I could find a way out of this with minimal embarrassment.

For the moment, the woman was mentally clear, and as she recalled her story for me she turned and asked, "Dear, I don't mean to be rude, but is someone coming that's *actually* going to help me?"

Man, I felt like shit.

Medical finally arrived, and I had to explain the lady's injuries; they could barely contain their laughter. This was getting worse, a lot worse.

The neighbors then came over, and again I had to recount what had happened.

Eventually, the people who watched over her showed up. They'd gone to a movie and thought that they could leave her alone for a short while.

I explained the door, as well as the screams and the injuries.

They didn't see any humor in the situation and explained to me that the woman was deathly afraid that Satan was coming to take her any moment now.

I left and wrote it up, hoping it would just go away...it didn't.

Dee got the medical team to tell her all about it, and she'd never let me forget it.

She gave me the nickname "Boot."

9 Born That Way

ONE NIGHT I WAS PATROLLING as the upper valley car, checking the canyon housing and surroundings in search of a mystery vehicle.

Residents had been reporting it as just parked in some remote area, usually at night, sometimes on private property, sometimes on federal forestland. So far, nobody had recognized it as being from the area.

Then one night, I finally came across the car hidden well back in the woods.

The windows were steamed up, and the occupants had no idea I was there.

I knocked on the window, and they rolled it down while frantically trying to get dressed—it was two men who I'd just seen locked in the 69 position in the back seat.

While they got dressed, I asked for their identification. At first, they didn't want to provide it, but they eventually did.

I didn't know the pair, both Hispanic males from the city.

I checked them for warrants, and they had none, so I filled out FI cards and told them that they were free to go—but not before advising them not to come back because the residents had spotted their car and complained.

About a year later, after I'd transferred to the city, I was dispatched to a gang fight.

Two rival sets were brawling, and we were called to clean it up and disperse the combatants. I went to deal with one group of gangbangers that was walking away from the scene but moving slower than we liked, and still talking shit to the gang that they'd been fighting with.

I recognized one of them from that night in the canyon; he was one of the occupants who had been steaming up the windows in the vehicle.

At first, I thought no biggie—but then when I went to help disperse the other group, there was the other guy from that night.

I was thinking, *how the hell did that happen?*

The two groups hated each other; it was multi-generational, and their gangs were at war every single night. How did these two gay guys from different gangs who wanted each other dead actually hook up? I couldn't even begin to imagine that conversation!

A few years later, I had the opportunity to ask one of them about it.

He said that they'd known each other in school before they'd cliqued up, each joining their respective gang. They'd admitted to each other that they were gay and mutually attracted to one another. They'd kept the secret hidden from everyone—including their fellow gang-bangers, who they backed-up each night; they were linked by gang loyalties, which were often more important than family ties, and they ran with homies who would have beaten them to death if they knew the truth.

So, when they met on the street, they'd talk a lot of trash and maybe fight but never seriously harm each other. They'd been lovers for years.

He said that was why they drove off to the canyon out in the county to meet; it was because "Nobody in the woods knew us."

He asked that I keep the secret since it would be doubly fatal for each of them: not only would they draw a beating from their homies for being gay. They'd also get it for being with a rival gang member.

I never told anyone, and I never used it against them to extract information; I figured they had more than enough to deal with.

Outliving Children

10

ADULT VICTIMS CAN SOMETIMES BE hard to sympathize with; some make choices that put them in a place where they knowingly become victims.

Not children; they're born helpless and grow up dependent, trusting, carefree, walking wide-eyed, innocent, and joyous through a world that will prey upon them once exposed. If they're left alone, unguided, or overlooked even for a second—it's over.

I wouldn't wish the painful aftermath from a child's death on my worst enemy.

That being said, not everyone should be allowed to have children. That becomes obvious on this job; so unavoidably, some children are born into lives where they just never have a chance.

Cammi Paulson was a 4-year-old girl who had been playing with friends at her grandfather's house and disappeared.

A 15-year-old boy, Daniel Wilkerson, claimed to have seen her picked up by some people in a car. He even helped out in the search for her.

This being one of my first cases as a city patrol officer, I was in field training with John Garcia. He was my mentor for years, and we called him "Father Time" for his calm, steady demeanor.

We went door-to-door, looking for the girl, literally going from room to room in every house and apartment in the central city. We searched for her all shift long for what I remember as several days; I'm pretty sure, though, that I'm blocking a lot of it out.

During the search, we fielded plenty of false reports from people who claimed to have seen her playing with their neighbors or walking past their house.

The last of the searching I remember was looking in garbage cans. We never said that we'd given up hope, but there was this unspoken feeling that it was time to search in garbage cans, in holes under houses, and anywhere a small body could be stuffed and hidden because we weren't going to find her alive.

This was before cell phones were everywhere, and I remember trying to control my panic and anxiety.

I felt somehow that my own baby girl was in danger, and I needed to call—but I couldn't; I had to keep on searching.

The search was methodical, systematic, and impressive; each city block was checked off when it was covered. I was actually very impressed by the organizational skills of the incident commanders. The communication actually went up and down the chain of command efficiently, unlike the cluster fuck I'd experienced at county. It felt like teamwork for once...figures that it would take something sick and twisted to bring a department together.

Eventually, Garcia came to me and said that the search had been called off.

The Wilkerson boy had confessed to killing and raping the little girl. He'd hidden her body in a plastic garbage bag and put her in the shed behind his house.

At the time, I didn't let on that I was really affected by this—but I struggled with my emotions, furious and stricken at the thought of what was done to this child.

I'd later read the entire report and talk to the veteran detective who got the confession so that I might learn everything I could from him. I wanted to be the guy who brought cases like this one to a close with a solid arrest.

He told me, like he later testified in court, that it was routine to question Wilkerson when it became apparent that he might have been the last person to see Cammi alive.

During the questioning, the kid's body language changed at one point; he suddenly stopped making eye contact and became distracted, acting like someone who was about to reveal something embarrassing about himself—not necessarily criminal.

The detective had seen this very thing happen many times before—a vulnerable moment—so he took a shot:

"Daniel, where's Cammi?"

He wasn't ready for the answer, and it shocked him when Wilkerson lost it and said that she was in the shed behind his house. Everything just emptied out of the kid after that.

I remember watching Wilkerson when they walked him through the station house, thinking that he wasn't noteworthy or unique; he was just a kid, like any other 15-year-old—except this one had raped and murdered a little girl.

I expected him to be so obviously a monster and a killer that I'd see it immediately, whatever "It" was...but there was nothing telling or unusual about him.

We went to a 7-11 afterward and got a drink, just sitting and slowly drinking in silence. No one said a word; we all just stared, thinking our own private thoughts.

People would come in and ask us how the search was going, asking if we'd found her yet. This was horrible. All I wanted to do was go be alone and deal with the mix of emotions and rage. We couldn't tell them she'd been found dead; they were controlling that through the press release.

We left the 7-11 and drove around for a while, just wanting it to be quiet and to get away from the public.

The prosecutors wanted to execute Wilkerson, but when they checked with the state Supreme Court they found out he was too young; he had to be sixteen to qualify for the death penalty.

His mother was a drunk and an addict, and his father was some brutal dickhead constantly in and out of prison, who beat and raped her regularly. That was about all we learned about the kid's home life. We were dealing with district court, not the behavioral research institute—and courts just establish blame.

I remember the kid's public defender making some whacked argument that he shouldn't be charged with rape; instead, he should be charged with desecration of a corpse since she was dead by then...just one of those glittering moments to remind him why he went to law school, I suppose.

These kinds of cases are the ones that really haunt you; as hard as you try to forget, it's always with you.

On another night, I was called to an address in the inner city. It was a basement apartment in the bottom of a fourplex, one of those old dilapidated places that no one cares enough about to keep up.

The occupant was a woman who had asked her new boyfriend to watch her infant son; she had to go to work and had no sitter. She'd dated the boyfriend for about six weeks and felt she could trust him with her son, plus she was in a bind. The boyfriend agreed, and she left.

What she didn't know, though, was that her boyfriend had a very low threshold for stress. She'd never seen him alone with the baby; she was always around and had no idea he couldn't care for the child alone.

According to the boyfriend, the baby started to cry and he couldn't comfort it or get it to stop crying. Eventually, frustration led to anger, and he reached a point where he couldn't stand it any longer—and he blew up.

At first, he said he started to punch the child—which only made the crying louder—so he threw the infant around the apartment and against the walls, and at one point he even dropkicked the baby to the ceiling like a football.

When he was finished, he just sat on the couch, staring at all the blood splatters and the pieces of the dead baby left everywhere; I tried my best to get him to do something, anything, to make any move that I could use as an excuse to seriously beat his fucking ass. But, he did nothing; with a flat affect, he just stared straight ahead and cooperated fully, and during the interview he started to talk about his own childhood and the abuse that he'd survived.

He said his mother whipped him with a coat hanger repeatedly and stubbed out cigarettes on his chest and back.

I didn't believe him until he lifted his shirt and showed me the worst scarring I'd ever seen; after that, I was quiet and in shock.

This wasn't what I wanted to see or believe. He had been tortured physically and emotionally and was a ticking time bomb that had finally gone off.

I pulled up his name on the computer and realized that I'd dealt with him before when he was a young boy. He'd been a runaway for several months, and I'd found him living on the streets, so I turned him over to juvenile court officials. At the time he was only ten years old, and he said he'd been living on the street for about five weeks.

A few years later, I ran into him again at a party, the people there wanting him removed; they were uncomfortable with how he was acting, bizarre and threatening. I checked, and he had a warrant for the sexual abuse of a child, so I took him to juvenile detention.

I asked him what had happened since I'd seen him last. He said he'd been in state care, bouncing from foster home to foster home, which he said he didn't like but that it was better than living with his mom.

I didn't see him again until the murder of the baby.

I didn't recognize him that night; life had hardened him and made him barely resemble the child I once knew.

He was booked on the murder of the baby and pled to the charges. His confession had sealed the case.

11 Devil Family

WORKING SWAT, OF COURSE, IS a glory gig that some cops aspire to; it certainly shines up the resume.

But it's also a job like any other, with petty in-house jealousies, grudges, cliques, and office politics—only magnified somewhat since everybody's armed to the teeth.

Like any job, some of my co-workers could be the subject matter of a behavioral pathology thesis—what with most of them being flat out nut jobs and eligible for any local psyche ward.

Henry Blair lived on the north end of the city in one of the newer but barely middle class areas lacking enough in destitution to be linked to the inner city.

One day, Henry had a small meltdown: his son came over to the house, and Henry came out and shot him with a rifle; he just shot his own son for no apparent reason and went back into the house.

A patrolman responding to the first call dragged the son to safety while Henry barricaded himself inside, and SWAT staged from a house nearby.

This call, however, was a really sweet set-up.

The staging house was really nice; we had full run of the place, with access to everything from the TV to the couches. Plus, we slept on carpeted floors and in chairs while we waited for Henry to be negotiated out of the house.

The snipers were out on rotating shifts while we on the entry teams were inside eating pizza, watching a big screen TV, and playing cards. I would say sleeping, too, but that's not really what it was.

When you're on that kind of call, you don't really sleep; you might catnap, but you can't really sleep. Henry had already shot one person, and we had to presume that he was ready to do it again—to one of us.

Usually, the situation is really tense, and the waiting can make you crazy if you don't have some way to release the tension.

I remember talking with one of the squad members, laughing about the mental image of sneaking over to the house, surprising Henry, and dragging him out of the house.

We envisioned tying him to a fence, bending him over, and yanking his crazy old man trousers down—then engaging him in candid anal rape while explaining the rules of "Team Bruised Anus."

We had to have a code word for our squad to identify itself to other teams as friendly if it ever came to the so-called thick of battle. Ours was "Black Angus," and that easily morphed into "Bruised Anus" for the purposes of payback on Henry; after all, it was his fault that we had to sit around in this house away from our families, forced to listen to the brass pontificate.

This career highlight of a SWAT assignment also included getting to know the brass in these calm times of waiting—and we always regretted it. We were surprisingly united on this point.

In police work, we have a saying: "Shit floats."

It means the good cops never rise through the ranks to float, so to speak, in the upper echelons. There's a reason that the saying continues to this day: shit continues to float.

As we sat laughing about Henry, the SWAT commander and the sergeant, the number two guy, came over and asked our opinion.

"I'm tired of waiting and talking the suspect out. I want some action," said top dog. "I want to go in and kick that old man's ass," added the sergeant.

At first, I thought they were joking—but they weren't.

I said I thought it would be best if we let the negotiators do their jobs. If we went in too early, the press might get wind of it—then all hell would break loose. They sort of nodded and walked away.

"What the fuck was that about?" I asked Jimmy, my fellow squad member.

He shrugged and said, "I don't know. They're bored. You know they're not right mentally anyway; no one wants to get into a fight like those two do. Why do you think they're nicknamed 'The Mini-Commandos?'"

"Christ, is *anyone* on this team normal?" I said, tired and a bit stunned. "Our squad leader reads Soldier of Fortune like it's a comic book, the commander is a fucking nut, the sergeant is an idiot douche, and here we are joking about sodomizing an old man bent over a fence," I said.

We started laughing again, mumbling, "Bruised anus...bruised anus."

Eventually, Henry was talked out of the house and arrested.

He'd fortified the place and tied the doors shut, and he'd made entry into the home possible through only one way so he could ambush whoever came in while he was behind cover; if we had stormed the house the way leadership wanted, we all would have been slaughtered.

This was a SWAT team that had what I considered an enviable record these days. Having never shot a suspect in twenty-five years of existence, we were the only SWAT team in the state left without a shooting.

You had to wonder, though, if that chapped the ass of the SWAT leadership. One more call would just about do it for me with this crazy ass bunch; this kind of "glory" wasn't what it was cracked up to be.

Demon Family 12

MAX ORTIZ LIVED ON THE west side of the city in an apartment on the end of a dead end street; "Over the viaduct," as they say, a rundown part of town that was seriously gang-infested.

He was supposed to be dealing cocaine out of the apartment.

Our briefing was that he was dangerous, armed, and that his whole family was armed as well. Max was a big dude back then and very intimidating, and the family name was well known on the streets. He had multiple weapons in the house—and even the elementary school-age kids were to be considered dangerous.

So, when we got ready to enter the apartment, the entire team was really jacked up.

I didn't know the kids, but later every one of the Ortiz girls would become informants for me—even against their own family.

We stacked up on the front door, prepared to do a no-knock search warrant and arrest everyone. I was third in line, and when we hit the door the front guy got hung up. So, the next guy opened the door per protocol, which made me the first through the door.

I went in and down the stairs as planned, running in to one of the girls and putting her on the floor, then handcuffing her.

The entry wasn't what we expected.

We were told that the entire family was streetwise and combative and that they'd be carrying weapons and were ready to fight; instead, there I was handcuffing a scared little girl who was crying, sobbing, and screaming for her life.

They had no idea what was happening, and I felt like an asshole.

I looked around and saw the rest of the team fucking this family up; they were afraid of going to battle with this "demon family" that didn't exist.

True, Max was a bad ass and his wife a prostitute rumored to carry a knife—but the girls were just little girls, and Max, Jr., was just a little boy.

After calming my suspect down by telling her that I wouldn't let her be harmed, I looked around the room.

One of our guys had his submachine gun to the head of one of the girls—and she was already cuffed.

The "battle" was over, the house secured, and all the suspects in cuffs. We were done with the entire operation in less than five seconds—yet he had his gun inches from her head, finger on the trigger, gun set on full auto, calling her a "fucking bitch" and screaming shit like "Who's the bad ass now?"

She was terrified, so I grabbed his weapon and yanked it away from her head—and instantly he was on me. "What the fuck are you doing?" he yelled.

As calmly as I could, I said that she was cuffed and not resisting. I then told him that he had his finger on the trigger and the gun pointed at her head—and that the gun was set to fire—cautioning him that he didn't want to have an accidental shooting of a cuffed suspect.

He just raged, "Never touch my weapon! NEVER!"

"Fuck you," I replied. "You're out of control. She's a little girl; grow the fuck up."

I got her up, and we left him glaring at me, speechless.

As we walked out, I watched him in case there was more.

He started to stare at the little girl, and his demeanor changed; suddenly, he decompressed like he was coming up from a deep-sea dive and finally saw that she was, indeed, just a helpless little girl.

In the SWAT vehicle on the way back to the station house, he stared at me a while, then finally said, "OK, you were right."

After that, we became friends briefly before he, too, left SWAT.

Years later, the Ortiz family moved into my patrol area, and I somewhat became friends with them—that is, as much as that was possible.

Max had beaten them often, and they were relieved whenever he was sent off to prison. The kids would mention that SWAT raid at times, the emotional scars obvious.

At first they'd laugh as they talked about how terrified they were, but the tears would always come—and I never told them that I was there.

13 Working The Crowd

ONE NIGHT, I WAS CALLED to the scene where someone had been shot and robbed in the central city.

The usual stuff, it gets routine after a while: looking for anyone who will admit to having seen or heard anything.

You have to understand that retaliation is a very real fear for the impoverished dwellers of our decaying urban cores.

After I spent some time interviewing witnesses who worked hard to elaborate on all the details they *didn't* know concerning what had just happened, I finally found a guy who would at least talk to me.

He said loudly that he'd never talk, no matter what—but his eye contact and facial expression said otherwise. He wanted me to act like I was arresting him, so I applied the cuffs and hauled him off.

Once we were outside visual range of his friends and neighbors, he told me what had happened, who the robber was, and even where the suspect lived. He even went so far as to sign an official statement at the police station. Ultimately, we located the suspect and arrested him, and I released the witness, thanked him, and went on to the next call.

After about a week went by, I was dispatched to a house to meet with a woman who'd been raped at knifepoint. She'd met the assailant at a house a few blocks away, and he'd walked her home, offering to keep her safe. She'd then invited him in for a drink.

When it came time for him to leave, though, he picked up a knife and told her that she was going to repay him for his kindness one way or another.

She had kids in the house and didn't want them to see or hear what was about to happen, so she convinced him to take her to her car, which was parked in the driveway.

It was inoperable, and she hoped that once they got there she might be able to talk him out of doing anything; unfortunately, when they got into the car he raped her anyway and left.

She told me she knew his name and where he lived—and guess who? It was Mr. Helpful from the armed robbery a week earlier.

I went to his place, and we talked amiably.

I thanked him for his help on the earlier robbery, then asked him to come down to the station to clarify some of the points in his statement.

Of course, this was all a ruse; once we were out of the neighborhood, I drove him past the rape victim's house and watched for his reaction.

He became upset and wanted to know where we were going. I told him that I just wanted to check on a friend who had called; I'd promised her that I'd drive by her house every once in a while.

Noticeably nervous, he was quite relieved when we got to the station. He was hoping to start talking about the robbery case, but that never happened.

I asked him if he knew the woman at the address that we'd just driven by, and he said that he'd never been there. I told him I had witnesses indicating otherwise, witnesses who had seen him walk her home—and that I knew he had, in fact, been there.

He agreed, trying to keep his cool. He said he misunderstood me; he'd been there, but just to walk her home.

I told him that I knew from his helping out on the robbery case that he was a good guy and that this woman was a little bit crazy.

He laughed and said, "She sure is. You don't know the half of it."

I asked him to explain that remark.

He said that after he walked her home, she wanted to have sex with him in her car and that she'd forced herself on him. Initially he refused, he said; it just didn't seem right. She was so insistent, though, and it seemed important to her, so he eventually gave in and they had sex. He did her a favor.

"That was it?" I asked.

He said yes and that he'd then left and gone home.

"What about the knife?" I inquired. "She said you had a knife."

He denied this, so I ran it all past him again, about what a good guy he was, taking a risk to help us out on the robbery, and would he consider helping us again to clear up this delusional woman's crazy story? I told him she had a cut from the knife and that she said he had a knife, so how did this happen?

He replied that she "liked it rough" and convinced him to hold a knife to her throat during his sloppy fucking. Her wish was his command. He said he must have slipped and accidentally nicked her.

I had him write down his admission to this "rough sex," then arrested him and booked him into jail on suspicion of aggravated rape.

Then, while at the booking center in front of other prisoners in the holding cell area, I thanked him for helping us with the earlier robbery case before I left—making sure they heard me, which was sure to make his time behind bars memorable; snitches are highly frowned upon in jail.

I suppose he thought he'd earned himself one free aggravated rape for helping solve a prior aggravated felony.

He pleaded guilty to the rape, and surprisingly we still got the conviction on the robbery; luckily, raping someone at knifepoint doesn't make you a liar in the eyes of the court.

Daywalkers 14

THERE ARE DAY PEOPLE, AND there are night people—and there's a huge difference.

The city, any city, transforms at night.

The world is quieter and still, in anticipation. It smells different and feels different, and your senses are heightened; you feel less numb and more aware.

There's a reason that predators in the wild choose the night, and human predators are the same, being naturally drawn to the cover of darkness with fewer eyes to see them.

That was my element, where we worked. We understood that even the day cops were different. They weren't as feral or aware; they didn't fit at night.

Night enhanced the battleground.

It was Us vs. Them, squaring off in the most rundown parts of the city, where economic pressures contort the already dysfunctional.

The 95% of the population that lived in the "Daywalker" world were gone; the killers and the people who took them on were out, holding ground until the sun started back around and the birds awoke, bringing the Daywalkers back out of their beds.

As the sky slowly brightened behind the mountains, the predators would retreat, and we'd go home as well.

One night, I was with Tim, a fairly new guy, working the graveyard.

It was around Christmas, and we were hanging out on a break in a convenience store parking lot when we got a report from a passerby hearing moaning coming from a backyard, an inner city alleyway area.

We laughed at first ("moaning?!"), thinking we were going to a call from some voyeurs who wanted us to witness them having sex.

It happens often enough: people make an anonymous call about something happening at their house—then get busy, screwing with their drapes or blinds open so we'll see them going at it when we roll up.

When we responded, we parked a couple houses down and walked to the address. It was an apartment complex.

We knocked, and no one answered.

We weren't even a little bit on edge; we were joking and laughing and talking quietly while we hung at the door.

We knocked again, and still no answer.

We checked back with dispatch, and they had no further information, so we were about to clear the call as unfounded. Before we did, though, we decided to go around to the back of the house—where we came across the body of a female, Aubrey Snyder.

She was lying face up, her blouse and bra pulled up to expose her breasts. One leg was folded under her body, and her bowels had evacuated, as they will in a sudden, violent death. Her head was covered in blood, and she wasn't moving.

I checked her pulse, and as I expected, she had none. I checked her eyes, and the pupils were blown. She was dead.

Staring, Tim had turned to stone. I don't know for sure, but I think it was his first dead body.

I started to talk him through it, explaining the scene and what we had to do, helping him to process the shock of what he was seeing.

This was an attack from someone very angry, a revenge killing—and it was a blitz attack on top of that. The killer knew her and was an organized offender, as they say in the reading material on homicide crime scenes; he exposed her chest in some kind of an attempt at misdirection because there was no sexual assault.

We called out what we had, letting the rest of the units on that night know what had happened.

The back door of the house was open, but there was nobody inside, and a search revealed nothing. The place wasn't ransacked, nothing was broken nor opened nor missing. The murder weapon had been removed from the scene, where a lot of leaves were covered with blood, and there was some splatter on the bricks of the house.

Later, investigators would learn that her estranged husband had killed her with the claw end of a hammer; he learned that she'd been having an affair with a cop from a smaller jurisdiction outside the city.

We protected the scene until detectives and CSI showed up. By then, our shift was over.

The case was really hard to make fit with the "real world" that we returned to; while Tim and I had talked and joked at the 7-11, Aubrey Snyder was getting her head caved in a couple blocks away.

This was the city, and after a while you just accepted the fact that violence was going to happen. We knew that, but leaving that scene left us with such a bleak feeling, like being short of oxygen or getting too much, unable to touch down again.

The kids were awake when I got home, and the wife was mad; I hadn't got home soon enough after working graves to help her with them in the morning.

We had a very large extended family, so the kids were still excited about Christmas. It took several days to visit everyone, so it was like Christmas week for the kids.

I was quiet, thinking about this woman who'd been beaten to death and trying to make that scene mesh with this one. That they were both in the same world on the same day, within an hour of each other, didn't work for me: a blood-soaked, shit-stained woman, beaten to death—and happy children, full of energy, laughing, giggling, and excited for more Christmas.

My wife at the time didn't want to hear about it, about why I needed a moment.

"Keep that horrible work stuff at work; don't bring it here to our home."

So, I just had to carry Aubrey around in silence.

Daywalkers rarely see mutual combat, and it can take the edge off in dealing with some victims, especially when they won't cooperate with police after a wicked bar fight.

One in particular was at a bar known for a lot of bar fights. More than the usual crowd had gathered for this contest, drawing numerous calls to dispatch since the bar was also on the main drag downtown.

I happened to be closest and rolled up first on the scene. The crowd was huge and there was much milling about, and when I pulled in most of them started to run.

A small group at the front waved me over.

A guy had a bar towel wrapped around his face and in a weird shape above his left eye. I asked what had happened, and the owner told me that the guy with the bar towel and another man had been in a fight earlier in the evening, with bar towel guy winning and the loser departing.

At closing time, the guy came back and wanted a rematch, but bar towel guy triumphed again even faster the second time around.

As he turned to walk away, one of the loser's friends jumped him from behind and stabbed him in the head with a "knife sharpener."

All the patrons were Hispanics, and their English wasn't perfect, so I wasn't exactly sure what they meant by "knife sharpener", even after asking several times.

So the guy with the bar towel unwrapped his head.

It turned out that it was actually one of those full-size knife sharpeners; the kind that looks like a metal rod that comes to a point that you run knife blades back and forth across—and it was jammed all the way up to the handle and downward into his left eye socket. The other end was sticking out below his jaw, near his throat.

Medical took him to the hospital, where he lost the eye, but surgery was able to repair the broken left side of his face. Even after all that, he refused to cooperate with our investigation, not giving us anything to go on; however, with so many witnesses, we were able to find out that the altercation was due to a dispute that originated in Mexico.

The two combatants were from rival states which had been in a feud with each other for years, a historical urban warfare. They'd been fighting and killing each other for some perceived slight of honor that had occurred decades ago.

God only knows what was coming next, as the witnesses assured us that the sharpener to the eye socket wasn't the end of it...more continued conflict was yet to come.

15 Skidmark

"SKIDMARK" WAS HIS NICKNAME; HIS real name was Skidlaski. That was what we called him when we thought about him—which wasn't much.

It wasn't because he smelled bad (which he did); we just had to consider him because he made our jobs more difficult.

He had zero common sense and no feel for the street.

He was one of those guys who thought he knew more than everyone else and wouldn't listen to anyone.

My first memory of him is of him pulling over a vehicle in a grocery store parking lot so that lots of people could see him. He'd been assigned to my area, so I had to take some calls with him.

It was Christmas Eve, and it's an unwritten rule between us cops that Christmas is hands-off; no bullshit tickets, no arrests unless it's absolutely necessary—and only when there's no other choice. We'd talk about it in briefing with no objections from the sergeants.

So Skidmark pulled over this vehicle and started running the occupants; son-of-a-bitch was digging for warrants—and he'd already violated the rule by stopping them.

I drove past to see that he had this station wagon full of wrapped presents and three scared little kids in the back; as I drove off, Skidmark waved at me as I passed as if he was thanking me for checking on him.

I left this bullshit scene and listened for the outcome of the stop on the radio: the plates on the station wagon had expired, and the mother was driving on an expired license.

Skidmark called for a wrecker and impounded the car with the gifts inside; he actually put the kids and the mom on the street on Christmas Eve. He did at least call someone to come pick them up after giving her a ticket...a regular St. Dick he was.

From that point on, I was done with him.

I cancelled him on every call; I wouldn't work with him.

He had a really fucked up way of seeing the world, which I couldn't understand and didn't want to. I became one of his most outspoken opponents in the department and on the street.

I started to hear from people in the area where we worked about how poorly he treated everyone and how they really didn't like him and couldn't talk to him, which was pretty much unraveling everything the rest of us had worked so damn hard to establish; it was blowing relationships and eroding all the trust that we were trying to build. He was constantly making our jobs harder by being such a horse's ass. He was a real cheese dick.

One night, Skidmark had arrested a guy for drinking beer in one of the city parks. He felt like he was cleaning up the area by arresting everyone for anything he could think of anytime they moved; like I said, he had no feel for the street.

We overlooked a lot of smaller crimes because we needed the cooperation of the residents of the city to land the bigger fish. Maybe you mention the statute of limitations, that we could get the charges filed anytime in the next two or four years, whatever it was; maybe you don't mention it at all if you don't need to.

Inner city dwellers knew about how the criminal justice system worked as well as we did.

Skidmark couldn't grasp this concept, though, and he arrested everyone for even the slightest of violations in order to pump up his stats.

In some misguided attempt to break up cliques in the department, management had come up with a shift bid system where the highest performers on each squad could pick their shift the following year. They called it the golden squad; we called it the golden shower squad. It didn't work, but it lasted for a long, long time.

New guys like Skidmark saw this as a way to get better shifts without having to pay their dues on the street like all the rest of us had.

He wanted to get off the graveyard shift as soon as possible; I, on the other hand, loved graves, particularly since my latest marriage was coming undone. It allowed me to avoid the wife and spend time with my kids.

On this particular day, Skidmark had arrested this guy for drinking in the park; it was under an obscure ordinance meant to help us keep the parks clear of drunks, not common citizens sharing a few beers while barbecuing.

The guy Skidmark arrested was pissed off, and Skidmark was talking shit to him as he was taking him to his car, telling him what a waste of a human being he was, a pain in Skidmark's fat ass.

He handcuffed him, put him in the car, seat belted him in, and locked the door. He then left to go back to the park to arrest a couple more guys he saw drinking there.

This was really stupid, not to mention a safety problem—a real potential for a cluster; any cop that's worked the streets will tell you that. You don't load up your car with drunks to take to jail just so you can get stats.

Skidmark arrested another guy and brought him back to his car—only to find it empty with the passenger door wide open; the first guy had unlocked the car and run off with his handcuffs.

The cuffs were your personal property back then. We had to buy them, and of course Skidmark always carried a lot of them.

He jumped on the radio, screaming for backup because he had an escaped prisoner. I didn't move; I just listened to the shit storm unfold and shook my head.

Several units looked for the guy for hours but couldn't find him. How impressive is that: shaking people down for details on the guy who stole an officer's cuffs?

I just stayed out of it. I didn't want anyone on the street to see me with this dickhead or associate me with helping him.

He finally gave up and took the rest of his catch to jail, then bitched for days about "that piece of shit who stole my cuffs" and how he'd get even. Gave his pitiful little life direction, I guess.

About a week went by, and I got a call to meet a woman I knew at her home.

When I showed up, she was sitting on the front porch with her son and daughter. She said that she wanted me to hear what her son had to say.

He was just a kid, maybe nineteen or twenty.

I listened, and he told me about how he was arrested and escaped with the officer's handcuffs. It was Skidmark's escaped bad guy!

My reaction wasn't what he expected.

The kid was all tense and edgy, and I think he expected to get hit or take a beating; instead, I started to laugh—and laugh hard!

"Really? That was you?" I asked.

He said that it was, and he recounted how Skidmark—he didn't know it was Skidmark, he called him "Officer Cheesedick" (quite funny, really)—made him angry talking down to him, so after he was left in the car he felt it was his duty to try to escape.

He also described how Skidmark had a distinctive odor and was fat and wheezed.

The kid said, "I felt like a bitch going down without fighting this guy."

I was laughing really hard by now at his descriptions, amazed that it was almost exactly how most of Skidmark's fellow officers felt about him.

However, his mother wasn't happy and didn't see the humor in it; she didn't want her son to feel that this was acceptable behavior. To hell with that.

I explained that "Skidmark" was his nickname and that he was exactly what her son had described—and although I didn't endorse his escape, I did understand it.

She asked, "What are you going to do now?"

I looked at the son and said, "Well, that's up to you. I don't wanna lose my cuffs. If you're gonna run, have at it, man. Go!"

He didn't move.

I told him that if he went with me, he'd go willingly, then gave him my cuffs and told him to put them on. His jaw dropped. He asked if I was serious.

"Yeah, man," I said. "You put them on, then you can show me how you got out of Skidmark's car."

He liked that idea. He was proud of the fact that he'd escaped. He even put them on behind his back.

I took him to the car, buckled him in, locked the door, and said, "Go!"

He was out in fifteen seconds.

I was seriously impressed with his method—which, for obvious reasons, will not be revealed.

I sat there with him and, with his help, figured out a way to defeat his escape. We then laughed and joked, talking and exchanging ideas.

Then I let him tell his mom goodbye, took him to jail, and booked him on the warrant of the escape charge against him. I told him that Skidmark was on duty that night. "He's gonna want to come talk shit to you. The cuffs you took were his favorite set," I said.

The kid said he thought maybe that explained why they smelled kind of odd.

"You don't still have them, do you?" I asked.

He said no, that he'd cut them off and thrown them away.

I called Skidmark on the radio and told him that his escapee had been booked into jail.

He replied that he was on his way to the jail; for him, this was personal. I warned the kid about him being on his way, then left.

Nothing ever came of it. Skidmark continued doing his thing; I just made a point of not working with him.

Tulips By Any Other Name Still Smelled Like Shit

16

THREE IN THE MORNING IS like some dead zone on patrol.

The bars have emptied out for the most part, and chasing drunk drivers home is pretty much over. The last of the debris from party time in private homes is still stumbling around, hoping not to get caught.

I first ran into this guy during that time.

Someone had walked through the park and thought he was dead, but he wasn't; he was just really drunk. I don't remember his first name, but his last name is Tulips. Seriously! He had the identification to prove it.

I woke him up and ran his identification, which I had to take from his wallet. He was too drunk to answer questions or even talk or get up on his feet; he just sat there mumbling while I ran the identification.

I learned that Mr. Tulips had an outstanding warrant, so I pulled him to his feet and walked him to the jail, which was nearby.

I made a tactical decision that I didn't want to put him in my car; he had an incredible stench of shit, urine, and some foul ass smell I couldn't recognize.

As we searched him at the jail, it turned out he had a colostomy bag. It hadn't leaked or spilled, but he wasn't very careful when he emptied it, and some of the contents had ended up on his clothing; thankfully, this time I was spared the "full blast of the bag." I booked him and left.

The correctional officers, on the other hand, were *not* happy.

They'd dealt with Mr. Tulips before, and they hated handling this guy because of the smell and the fact that he'd lay on the bag when he passed out—causing it to burst.

They also told me, for future reference, that it wasn't wise to call him "Tulips"; he could fly into a rage at hearing the name pronounced as it was written. He preferred a French-sounding pronunciation, and he found "Twallup" more aristocratic. (Never mind that he smelled like shit; in his mind, he was French.)

About three months later, I was called to the downtown park near the jail again.

It was 3 a.m. again, and there was another report of a man possibly dead. The caller said the man looked beat up; he was bleeding from a small head wound and lying in an awkward position, and the caller couldn't tell if he was breathing.

I arrived and found that it was the French Mr. Tulips again. He'd been robbed, his few possessions stolen, and this time his colostomy bag had ruptured. He was covered in shit from head to toe, and in his drunken stupor he'd rolled around in it; it was all pretty disgusting.

I requested medical and advised dispatch of Mr. Tulip's condition—and medical wasn't happy when they arrived; gagging and dry heaving, they treated his injuries while I watched, then they released him back to me.

I walked him to the jail again; he had another warrant for missing the court appearances from his last arrest. He'd also been given community service and hadn't completed it.

The correctional officer was the same guy as the last time, and he also wasn't happy. He put Tulips in a holding cell and hosed him off—literally.

I left, feeling bad for the correctional officer. The French man reeked like no other that night, but he was aware enough for me to test the "Tulips" pronunciation warning.

I pronounced his name as "Tulips" (like the flowers) when I addressed him, and he stopped and looked at me—glaring real rage in his eyes, his shit-soaked hair hanging in his face.

"Don't ever refer to me by that name again," he said.

He was ready to fight, but my curiosity was satisfied, so I backed off immediately and apologized profusely—not wanting to battle a shit-soaked man.

In my mind, a shit-covered man had a lot of liberties. He could say almost anything he wanted, and I'd agree with him; I didn't want to have to touch him—much less fight him. I never saw him again after that.

I did, though, hear Skidmark sign out on him one night.

Tulips was drunk in the park, and Skidmark was hunting his stats again. He was describing the guy being covered in shit and having a colostomy bag.

I came over the radio and told Skidmark that the guy's name was Tulips. I said that he liked to be referred to as "Mr. Tulips" and that if he didn't want the remaining contents of the bag to get all over him, he'd be wise to refer to him as such.

A few moments later, Skidmark was screaming for back up; Tulips was fighting him, and Skidmark was all covered in shit.

I was laughing so hard, I had to pull over.

17 It Can Make You Crazy!

ONE NIGHT, WE WERE SEARCHING for a guy after a domestic was reported.

The caller said a man had beaten a woman, threatened her with a gun, then left.

We caught him running around an industrial area, and the veteran sergeant on duty was summoned since he was known for handling difficult suspects.

They called in Sgt. Kenny Duke (nicknamed the "Mad Monk" for his monk-like appearance) because the suspect was being a complete ass, a real fuck stick.

I then heard him calling for an additional unit, which caught my attention.

The Mad Monk never called for more back up than he needed; he was one of my mentors, and he was great at talking down suspects and rarely involved in scuffles, even though he could take on anyone if he needed to.

Being a power lifter and runner, he was very fit; I once saw him pick up a 185-pound man with one arm and shake him.

Duke was fifty-eight at the time, having turned down a lieutenant's promotion to stay on patrol on graveyards with us.

When I rolled up, they had the ass clown surrounded, and they were trying to talk him into revealing where the gun was.

He was arrested, but no gun had been recovered, and our fear was that he'd dropped it or stashed it somewhere along the way as he fled. There was a reason for our anxiety.

Earlier that summer, some kids had found a gun which had been used by gang members in a drive-by. The gang bangers threw it out of the car after the shooting, and responding units were unable to locate it.

A couple days later, some neighborhood kids found it and thought it was a toy. One of the children had been accidentally shot in the head and killed.

At the moment, this was the biggest concern that the entire shift had. We didn't want kids finding another discarded handgun.

Sgt. Duke gave up trying to talk to the guy; he had this incredibly aggravating demeanor, which immediately set everyone on edge.

Duke waved me over and said, "Slick, can you talk to this guy? You're the calmest of us right now. He's really worked the squad up, and we can't be civil with him. You try to find out where the gun is, and we'll walk away and leave you two alone."

I agreed to try.

The guy was extremely combative, but I eventually calmed him down and tried to get the location of the gun out of him.

He was over-the-top irritating and foul-mouthed. It wasn't his swearing so much as the way he did it; he truly meant it when he said, "Fuck you"—conveying real hatred and animosity.

I thought I would explain why we were so concerned about the gun, thinking it would change his mind; it would have little effect on his prosecution, though, since we had multiple witnesses who would testify to seeing the gun anyway. I explained about the kids and our little guy who'd been accidentally shot in the head and killed.

This cocky ass looked me straight in the eye and said, "I don't give a fuck if some little Spic kid shoots himself in the head. Why the fuck would I care?"

I don't remember much after that—but I do remember seeing red in my vision, like the red filter effect on a camera.

Duke said that I slammed his head hard onto the trunk of the car and broke his nose. He said I slammed it so fast, he could hardly see the guy; he was just a blur. Duke came running, as did the other guys.

I rarely lost it, ever. I was one of the calmest guys on the department; I talked a lot more than most, and if I did fight, it was fast, over quickly, and always started by the other guy.

This guy, though, had gotten to me instantly.

I had him by the hair, ready for face slam number three, and I do remember violently whispering to him to tell me where the gun was or I'd kill his ass.

It was surreal, like I was watching a movie of someone else slamming this guy into the trunk of the patrol car. I was in a rage. Blood was everywhere, and Duke told me to leave.

He then had another guy take the car and wash it while yet another guy took face plant to the hospital to be treated. I never heard a word about this from anyone.

It was funny, though; people treated me differently after this. I was given a lot of room from the people I worked with.

They were just different and seemed almost afraid of me—except for the Mad Monk. He just laughed when he said to me later, "I thought I was just having a bad day—but shit, he got under your skin, too, and fast. I've never seen you mad like that."

Mad not so often, but annoyed plenty of times.

Eventually, I moved over to detectives and another patrolman took over my old area. The guy was something of a rival; I'll call him "Divot" since "Gash" could be misunderstood.

Divot said he'd take over my "shit hole" of an area and "turn it around." This made me laugh; I couldn't wait to see him try.

I was out in my unmarked car one of those very first nights on my new assignment, learning the ropes, when a call came over of shots fired in my old area.

Divot took the call and said he was en route, but he was slow, and as usual I arrived first.

I found a guy lying face down in the driveway of a home with a huge bullet hole in his back, and it was a through-and-through.

He'd also been run over several times and left in the driveway of the home next to a small market. Someone really wanted to make sure he was dead.

I was alone there for some time before I finally called Divot on the radio and asked his location. He replied that he was still at the police station; he was probably "polishing the brass" but would be en route as soon as he could.

I replied that I'd just wait and secure the scene of his homicide for him while he finished his real work at the station house. He finally got off his fat ass and actually showed up.

We exchanged a few words about his ability to turn this shit hole area around with his amazing work ethic, and finally someone separated us.

The victim had been shot with a .44 caliber handgun during an argument with his ex brother-in-law. The ex brother-in-law then backed his car over him in the driveway, stopped and pulled forward, drove over him again, then backed up to run over him one more time before leaving the area.

Patrol units saturated the area looking for witnesses, eventually turning up two people who said that they witnessed the entire thing.

After they watched this guy get blown away right in front of them, then repeatedly run over by a car—they just stepped over the body and went into the nearby store to buy cigarettes. After they bought their smokes, they returned again—stepping over the body on their way home.

They were completely unmoved by the experience of witnessing the murder—and this is the reality of the central city; the people there are harsh and survival-oriented, with violence being a daily event.

Divot cleaned up the scene, and I assisted the homicide detectives assigned to the case.

The owner of the little store came out and demanded that we get the investigation off his property; his parking lot was part of the crime scene, and he felt strongly that we were slowing his business down by being there. It took a threat of going to jail for criminal interference with a public servant to shut him up.

The shooter left the state, and after eventually getting arrested in New Mexico for intoxication and mistakenly released, he entered Mexico. As far as I know, he was never caught.

Your mentality as a cop seriously becomes a lot like combat, like going to war with the walking shit bags that prowl the streets at night, gang rapists, drug dealers, and killers. You learn to own the shit that happens, and you want to make them pay for what they've done; it's yours to own and take responsibility for.

Daywalkers don't realize that.

They see it as a job—but it isn't a job; it's personal.

It's a chess game with these colossal fuckers, and the rules are stacked against you. Things go down right in front of you, and you take out those responsible, taking them right off the street—then they make bail and wave "Hello" the next day. Then it's three months, six months—even years—as their case winds through a courthouse.

Building up like a bomb ready to explode inside of you is the feeling that the courts are against you, the laws are against you—and yet somehow you're supposed to bring the wolves to justice and protect the sheep.

Let's Go For A Ride 18

I HAVE MY DARK SIDE, my evil side. We all do; it's just a matter of what will bring it out in us—and watching helpless people being beaten brings it out in me.

I had a recurring domestic in an apartment building in one of the dilapidated parts of town no one cares about. A middle-aged woman named Mary lived in the basement on the right hand side with her boyfriend.

The boyfriend's name escapes me, but what I do remember was that he was a mean drunk.

They both liked to drink, and I think Mary was on Social Security for some type of disability. Basically, he was living off her—so he was impressive almost immediately.

The guy was constantly beating the hell out of Mary, and I'd take him to jail—only for him to get out, come back, and convince her to take him back.

The "Honeymoon" period is a classic pattern. Some try to tell you it's the thin line between love and hate crossing back and forth, and all that passion—but it's bullshit.

It apparently has something to do with testosterone: battered women shelters tend to fill up after the opening weekend of the deer hunt, the day after Super Bowl Sunday, and just after Christmas for good measure.

Some women will take it as long as they can (in some sick way, some honestly like the abuse), especially if the dickhead is the father of her children. He's so good during the honeymoon stretch; the man who beat her self-esteem into splintered bones is the one who then lifts her back up. It's a cycle regular as clockwork.

Mary's guy would be good for about six weeks, and then beat her ass again.

I'm surprised I can't remember his name; we spent so much quality time together. I used to check in on Mary to see how she was, which only angered the shit bag more. He'd get all pissed off and accuse me of getting blowjobs from her when he wasn't around. He was an evil fuck.

After getting a call from her one night, I went by.

Once I arrived, I entered the apartment at her request.

He was drunk and had broken every one of the fingers on her right hand. He did it one at a time, apparently concerned that someone might mistake him for a human being.

"Show him your fucking hand, you bitch!" he yelled at Mary; told you: supreme dickhead, this guy.

She was in tears, wailing kind of quietly, her fingers sticking out in all directions. Even Stephen King didn't think of this for one of his horror movies.

He was strutting around the apartment, acting defiant, talking all kinds of shit, chain smoking, and throwing things around—and I was starting to get crazy angry.

"What happened to her hand?" I asked, thinking about my next move.

He said that she was getting mouthy and that he started "breaking fingers to shut the fucking bitch up." He said it as an answer to me, but he yelled it at her.

I'd had enough.

I cuffed him and started to haul him out of the apartment.

He said, "This again, Slick? ("Slick" is one of my nicknames.) You know that this is a waste of time. I'll do what the fuck I want.

That bitch loves me. She can't do without my cock. Trust me, she loves my shit."

I opened the door to my patrol car and slammed his head hard against the doorpost twice as he got in; needless to say, he was stunned.

"Bitch, I will have your fucking job! You're gonna be begging for fucking food when I'm done with you!"

I seat-belted him in the car, then pulled up to the door and told Mary that we were going to jail and that she needed to get her hand looked at. She didn't want me to call for medical because an ambulance ride was too expensive. She said she'd get it looked at as soon as possible and thanked me.

The entire way to jail, he was still talking shit.

I knew I had to find a way to reach this shit bag, or he'd end up killing Mary. The system wasn't working, and he feared nothing...it was time to change that.

I drove past the jail, heading west out of town.

"Hey, fuckface," he said, "you missed the jail; it's back there."

I stared straight ahead and didn't comment for a while until he ran out of steam, making him wonder what the fuck was going on.

Calmly and quietly, I said, "You're right. You *WILL* go back and hurt her again. So, I'm taking you out west. I'm gonna blow your fucking brains out, bitch. Then I'm gonna dig the bullet out of your skull, cut your fucking hands and feet off, and leave you there to fucking rot. I'm taking you to the animal dump to die like the shit bag you are."

Far out on the west side of the county, there was an animal dump where farmers and ranchers disposed of their dead livestock, like cattle, horses, and pigs.

I could tell that he was scared now, but he was trying to stay calm; by the time we got to the dump, though, he was crying, sobbing hysterically.

It was pitch dark, and there were no headlights to tell him that someone would come save him.

When I got him out of the car, I dropped him face down next to a rancid, bloated, rotting cow carcass that had been dumped—and he started sobbing even more hysterically, spitting out the dirt and pieces of decomposing flesh that he'd inhaled when he hit the ground.

Screaming that he was sorry, he promised he'd never do it again and that if I let him live he'd move out and swore I'd never see him again.

I let him beg and plead, smelling the shit and the dead animals rotting around him; I liked seeing him in fear for once.

I got out a sharp knife that I kept in my trunk and made sure that he saw it, then laid out a tarp and gloves next to him.

I also had some duct tape and needle-nose pliers; I really had no use for the tape, but the effect was brutal cool. I kept at my preparations quietly, and by that time he was making little whimpering sounds while saying "please...please," sort of gurgling over and over.

"See...you can be polite," I said.

I put on the gloves, picked up the knife, and stood in front of him for a minute; he actually started shaking.

"Well, that should about do it. Say goodbye, fuckhead," I said, then put my gun to the back of his head.

He was kneeling and kept repeating, "Please give me another chance" and "I'll never bother her again" over and over.

"Why should I believe your punk ass, bitch?"

"Because I mean it this time," he answered. "I mean it. I see that you're serious. I won't go back and touch her—I swear."

"Pinky swear?" I said, smirking.

Crazy? Maybe.

With that, he toppled over sideways, sobbing and shaking like he was having a seizure; he was almost epileptic, thrashing in the mud and shit and rotting entrails.

I picked him up, slammed him against my car, and grabbed him by the throat. "If I let you live, I'll never see you again, right? Because if I do—it's on, motherfucker. No one will ever find you...*ever*. You don't have to do anything to her; all you have to do is show up and let me see you—and I will fucking *end* you. Do you get that?"

He said that he did.

Suddenly falling quiet, his eyes started blinking wildly, darting about in shock; he thought I was going to kill him and that his life had ended.

After cleaning him up a bit, I put him in my car, then drove him to the jail and booked him. I never saw him again.

For some time after that, I checked on Mary almost daily.

One day, she said that he came back and got his stuff from the apartment. He told her he was sorry, really sorry, and that he was leaving. He was wrong for hurting her, and maybe he wasn't the right guy for her. He said that he had to leave and that he couldn't stay. She said he was acting really terrified, jumpy as hell and looking out the windows, and that he left right away.

She smiled at me and said she didn't know what I'd done, but he couldn't get out of there fast enough. She moved out of my area a short time later.

I kept in touch with her enough to know that she was living a much happier life after this guy had his epiphany...being a brutal, psychotic bastard works sometimes.

19

Some Nights Were Different

WHO SAYS COPS DON'T HAVE any fun?

One night, I arrested a guy for public intoxication. I'd been dealing with him on a regular basis: he would pass out on people's porches and in their front yards, then I'd get a call from freaked out homeowners about the drunken stranger on the porch or in their lawn chair, and I'd take him to jail to sober up.

However, this particular night I thought I'd have some fun tormenting him in his inebriated state: he was falling down drunk, so I put him in my car, then proceeded to drive backwards to the jail.

It was one of those late nights/early mornings when the only people on the streets were newspaper carriers and cops.

At first, he didn't pick up on it; then he realized something was very wrong but that it was probably in his own head.

I continued to play it off like we were going forward, talking to him like nothing was wrong.

I drove with my mirrors and kept looking forward as much as possible—and the illusion worked.

"I really got to quit drinking," he kept saying.

After about a mile, he closed his eyes and told me, "Officer, I know that you said we're going forward, but I swear to you it looks like we're going backward."

It was probably one of the few times someone was glad to arrive at the county jail.

Later that night, my sergeant asked me quite calmly why I was driving backwards through the central city.

"Man, I'm glad you never picked me up drunk," he said.

I never saw my serial drunk again. I don't know if he quit drinking, but I like to think that maybe he did.

Some officers are just lightning rods for cops' twisted sense of humor, and Sgt. Gus was one of those targets.

We'd just finished a big case, an ambush just outside the mall downtown. One gang had crept up on another and emptied a handgun into their car while they were trapped in traffic, waiting for a stoplight; two in the car were wounded.

The attack happened in broad daylight, so we had to solve it fast. In less than twenty-four hours, the suspects were in custody, locked up with enough evidence that we didn't even need to try for confessions.

Gus was debriefing us, making sure he had all the details of the shoot and the arrests before he called the duty lieutenant whose shift had just ended a little earlier.

The duty lieutenant, or watch commander, had to be brought up to speed in case the media called, as lieutenants are the only officers authorized to give public statements.

Gus thought of himself as an efficiency expert.

He had all kinds of phone lists miniaturized and laminated in his wallet, and he'd pull one out and show it to us, making sure we saw how efficient he was. (He wrote with excellent grammar and lovely penmanship.)

We rolled our eyes and waited for him to finish showing off his little wallet cards. In light of all this, we figured he could make the call, using the numbers on his little lists.

This is where he really blew it badly.

Gus and the Chief were always at odds—and definitely not friends.

Gus had applied for the Chief's position when it had opened up some eight months earlier, competing with the man who was now his boss. On top of all that, they'd already been adversaries in the department for years.

Gus thought of himself as an intellectual cop, while the Chief saw himself as a military man by way of his Army reserve experience. They couldn't have been more opposite in their outlook and approach to police work, as well as life in general.

The Chief hated Gus, who was overweight and a prankster, never serious, and always joking. He even moonlighted as a comedian at a local comedy club. The Chief, however, almost never laughed—ever.

So Gus calls who he thinks is the duty lieutenant (who has the same first name as the chief) and starts his usual joking and talking shit.

He starts saying he's surprised that James is asleep already, then goes on about how James is no doubt tired from banging his new girlfriend, asking if she's as hot as she appears to be. He then makes comments about how he imagines she performs in the sack; she was a dispatcher who we all knew to be a bit wild.

So he continued to ramp it up, still not realizing that it was Chief James he was talking to.

He even told him, "At least you're not at home with a ball gag in your mouth, taking it up the ass like the chief...his wife runs him *and* their house."

Gus actually started picking up speed then, noting, "Mrs. Chief probably keeps a strap-on in the drawer by the bed, and no lubricant—just like the chief likes it."

He started laughing his ass off at the picture he was painting for Lieutenant James, believing it all quite funny—when all of a sudden he stopped and his demeanor suddenly changed.

He instantly sat up straight as a rail and said, "Yes, Sir," then "Yes, Sir" again, giving a quick brief of the shoot and apologizing profusely "for any inconvenience."

Gus then hung up (looking like he was about to hurl), put his head down on the desk, and said, "Oh shit...I am so fucked...oh God...I am so fucked."

He was always pulling pranks, so we just thought he was messing with us. We weren't buying his act, so he stood up and screamed at us, saying, "This isn't fucking funny! I'm serious."

Still not believing him, we asked what had happened.

He slowly, painfully said that he'd mistakenly called Chief James instead of Lieutenant James.

We all looked at each other in shock, thinking about what he'd said in that conversation—then we all burst out laughing. We laughed so hard, some of us grabbed trashcans while others dry heaved, coughing, choking, and trying to breathe.

Gus stormed out of the office, leaving us there with tears streaming down our faces. He and the Chief had many fun times together, but none of them quite got Gus fired.

Six months later, for instance, Gus and the Chief had another warm exchange.

Gus was having an affair. He'd been married for some time and loved his wife, but he had this low self-esteem to deal with.

He had a part-time job at a local department store, working as their security chief. One of the girls there liked his sense of humor and was going through a divorce, and she made it clear to him that she was up for whatever he had in mind. This was a first for Gus; he was really overweight and dumpy looking, so he ran with it.

One day he took her to a city park, a popular one with a large pond that drew in lots of geese and ducks, as well as a large parking lot that drew in a lot of thieves.

Gus didn't know that the major crimes division had staked out the parking lot for a series of car burglaries and that they were currently running surveillance with cameras.

So here came Gus, skipping and jumping over rocks in full frolic while carrying the picnic basket he'd packed for his lady love on the down low.

The major crimes detectives were working hard, catching every moment, kiss, butt fondle, and tit grab, and when they finished they packed up and left—but not before dropping a note on Gus' car (unsigned, of course) about the fine pictures they had of him and the girl...cop humor is brutal.

Gus was beside himself. He didn't know what to do or who had taken the questionable pictures.

The state police academy had been known to pull an officer's certification over extramarital affairs; it was an urge that came and went arbitrarily based on politics, so you never knew what could happen.

Gus fell back on the engrained experience of confessing and explaining his actions—but who was he to confess to?

He decided that he should confess to Chief James since he believed the Chief had the department detectives conduct surveillance of him for his illicit affair, and he did just that, requesting a meeting with the chief and the assistant chiefs (his need for penance was just that strong).

He went into great detail, telling them everything—including every time he met with the girl and everything they did—confessing that he knew how wrong it was but that he couldn't help himself.

I heard that the chief was in shock and asked Gus why he was telling them all this, to which Gus replied by outlining the picnic and the note left on his car; he felt sure that the chief had ordered the surveillance, and he wanted to come clean about everything.

The chief called him a fool, saying he couldn't care less about his affair. He then told him that he knew nothing about it until Gus turned himself in, then ordered him the hell out of his office.

I was walking past as Gus departed the chief's presence; he had the same "I am so fucked" look on his face as he had the night that he made the accidental phone call to the chief.

I later found out why and made sure that all the guys in the unit heard about it, after which we left him little picnic baskets with notes attached on his desk every now and then. He didn't think it was funny—but we did.

A few months later, Gus got me back in short order.

He'd fallen down a rickety flight of stairs during a bust of a dope house, and he needed a little patching up at the hospital.

In his report on his injuries for the case file, he wrote only one sentence: "Officer Fortier pushed me down the stairs."

I had some awkward moments detailing that one for the lieutenants, trying to prove a negative before Gus updated his report a few days later. I didn't think it was funny—but he did.

Sgt. Kenny Duke was the master of the deadpan delivery.

He was nicknamed "The Mad Monk" for his appearance and quiet demeanor—that is, until you pissed him off...then, "The Mad Monk" came out.

One night in midnight briefing, Kenny said that for years when the phone would ring and his wife answered, he'd break out in a sweat, wondering if it was a girlfriend calling who had somehow obtained his home number. He'd wait, listening to the tone of her voice, awaiting any clue that he might have to leave or prepare to defend himself in case she came for him.

His wife was a volatile woman, prone to scream and rant—but that was part of what he liked about her. That really hit me: stone-cold Kenny Duke sweating at the sound of a phone ringing.

He said one night he came home and had no early warning.

After thinking that he was out all night "womanizing," his wife was waiting for him with his service revolver. She shot at him six times, emptying the gun; she tried to kill him.

In that straight-faced delivery of his, Kenny said it instantly occurred to him that he was really glad he hadn't taught her how to shoot.

It also occurred to him that he might want to move out or at least store his gun where she couldn't get at it.

He said he wasn't entirely sure that she hadn't hit him, so he checked his chest and legs, feeling for blood. All six shots came in a small room at point blank range, but somehow she'd missed. He said he took her a little more seriously after that.

It was all in his delivery.

We couldn't help laughing, imagining Sgt. Duke dodging bullets while trying to reason with a crazed wife.

That story really struck a nerve with us, probably because we'd all been there at some point—and most of us were still living that nightmare to one degree or another.

20 Outranked

SGT. LEEDS WAS ALWAYS TALKING about his quest for a spirit animal guide.

While waiting for the owner of a building we'd cleared to show up and turn off the alarm, Leeds started telling us this story.

He'd been reading Indian lore on how to go about getting a spirit animal guide; he wanted to commune with the spirit world to get out there and mingle with the dead.

As he spoke, emotion made his voice crack a little.

He said he needed guidance from something "appropriately carnivorous"; after all, he was a warrior. He was also concerned that it was taking so long for this spirit animal to reveal itself to him.

Setting up his primitive camp alone, he'd actually sit in the mountains east of where we were for days at a time, squatting out in the elements, dressed in his buckskins and moccasins with warrior paint on his face, fasting, chanting, and beating on a drum.

He told his wife he was off camping so she'd think he just needed to get away; little did she know, he was a crazed, drooling, wannabe shaman.

So far, there was nothing. No sign; not even a curious coyote offering a fish or the wind in his hair, whispering ancient messages. Hell, even a tap on the shoulder would've been nice.

His Irish-Catholic roots hadn't done it for him: there was no animal soul included in that particular map to spiritual fulfillment.

He really worried about his spirit guide not being an "appropriate" animal; he thought himself too manly to accept a docile animal, such as a ground squirrel.

Just then, the owner of the building showed up.

It turned out to be just a routine false alarm; we'd checked the building, and the alarm had proven unfounded.

"Who wants the wisdom of a ground squirrel?" said the sergeant as he got back into his car, leaving us to clear the call. "I'm hoping for a bear or a wolf, maybe an eagle."

We just stared as he drove off; shit-faced drunks we caught pissing in the park didn't talk this crazy shit.

He was bat shit crazy, like the night he matched testosterone levels with a group of "pee wee" gang bangers just getting into the life.

He and some of the patrolmen (his "followers," as we called them) had a group of the youngsters cornered in an elementary school parking lot. I'd heard them all sign out at the same time, so I knew something was up.

When I got there, Leeds was standing in the middle of the group of 11- and 12-year-olds.

It was late at night, and he'd thrown down his spare nightstick and dared each member of the group to pick it up and fight him.

The kids on the street aren't that naïve; you don't survive on the street being that stupid.

The reality was, Leeds was a nightstick instructor and also trained in martial arts, so any fight with an adult would've been no contest— let alone a kid. None of the bangers went for it, so Leeds called them cowards and "limp dicks," then stomped off.

It was a set-up: not only would they have gotten their asses kicked, but he'd also have cause to arrest them since threatening someone with a weapon is actually something we arrest people for all the time.

I'd asked around about Leeds and found out that he was connected at the hip with one of the assistant chiefs. They were allies who worked together to further their careers at the expense of others, partnering in many internal investigations and manipulating the facts in ways to target officers they just didn't like who didn't have the sense to play along with the prevailing winds.

Most people were reluctant to talk about him, but I did hear from one lieutenant who'd been on an awards evaluation committee.

In a situation with a man with a gun, the guy had drawn down on Leeds, catching him off guard. The suspect pulled the trigger, but it hadn't gone off. Leeds thumped the hell out of him, and submitted himself for a Medal of Valor.

The first go-round, the medal was refused.

The awards committee felt that he shouldn't be awarded for making a mistake that almost got him shot: Leeds had bullied the guy—as was his style—instead of using accepted arrest control techniques.

After Leeds went to the Chief and complained that he'd actually been quite heroic and deserved some recognition, the Chief asked the committee to find some way of recognizing him.

Eventually, the committee ended up giving Leeds the lesser Medal of Merit.

The officer who told me about it resigned from the committee; he felt it was a slap in the face of the officers who'd actually earned their medals. This kind of shit went on in the department all the time.

In another incident, two young kids were walking down the street at 2 a.m., carrying stereo speakers. It was only late spring, and gang activity had started up early with car prowls, thefts, fights, and shootings. With tension already up, the department was bracing for a long summer, so we checked it out.

I arrived at the same time that Leeds rolled up and I started talking to one of the kids while he had the other.

Then Leeds said to me, "I'm tired of this fucking shit. These little fucking Mexicans are gonna learn a lesson tonight."

"What the hell are you talking about?" I said. "They're walking with stereo speakers. You don't know if these are stolen—and if they are, from where."

"Fuck that. I'm tired of this shit. These spics are controlling the streets, and it's time we did something about it."

He took his kid behind his patrol car and cuffed him, then started kicking the hell out of him. I could hear the kid crying, obviously getting hurt, so I cuffed my guy, put him in my car, and told him not to try to get out—no matter what.

I then locked the car as Leeds started coming for him.

"Get that spic out of your car," he barked.

I said "No, it's not gonna happen; he stays where he is."

Leeds started pounding on my car, pulling on the door handles and screaming at me to open it up.

I responded by saying, "That was pretty impressive how you kicked that little kid's ass after you handcuffed him. I didn't realize you were so afraid of Mexicans."

Leeds whirled around, his attention on me now, and we shared a few quiet moments as other cars (not necessarily his followers) were rolling up on the scene.

I was able to explain clearly that he shouldn't do anything like that in front of me again.

I said, "I'm not to be trusted if you and your redneck fuck friends are gonna fuck up little Mexican kids. Are there any questions? Make sure the word gets out, dickhead." Then I left.

Leeds got his guy charged with resisting arrest.

I took mine to his home and dropped him off, bearing new tales of some white cops that are crazy—but maybe not all of them.

I'd heard that he'd done that a lot, earning a reputation on the street for bullying Hispanics. He hated Mexicans, even if they were Nicaraguan, Cuban, Dominican, or Guatemalan—it didn't fucking matter to him.

The reality was, if too many witnesses were around, he'd just yell; if no witnesses were around, he'd slap them around, then take out the stick and beat on them.

Another night, Leeds was screaming on the radio for back up; his tendency toward beating Mexicans was coming back around to bite him in the ass.

He'd gone in on a bar check alone, which was unheard of. On top of that, it was a Hispanic bar where his reputation for racism had preceded him.

Now was the time for payback, and they were kicking the hell out of him.

They'd locked the doors of the bar, and he was on the radio saying that the whole bar was against him and that he was fighting his way to the door.

I was a little surprised at the lack of responses from officers saying that they were en route—including me; maybe I wasn't the only one tired of his stupid shit.

When I did get there, he came flying out the door, his hair messed up and shirt torn; the dickweed had survived somehow, and he started trying to get back inside once he saw that other cars had finally rolled up...too bad the bar occupants had locked the door.

Leeds then put on the radio that he wanted officers to go to the back door to keep them all inside the bar.

With their revenge taken, the bar patrons wisely knew they had to depart since they'd just gone the rounds with a uniformed sergeant—and they all somehow made it out that back door.

Leeds came around back, and he was pissed that we hadn't "kept all those greasy fucking spics in the bar so I could kick every one of their asses."

I asked him how come the whole bar had decided to kick his ass? I knew why, but I just wanted to hear what he had to say.

He said that when he went in, some guy was staring at him. No one would speak English, so he just knew they were planning something. He walked up to a guy staring at him and asked what his problem was.

The guy said, "No hablo ingles," then Leeds called him a spic and flipped the cowboy hat off his head. (Seriously, this was the stupid kind of shit he did.) The guy got pissed off, and the fight was on with the whole bar.

Leeds was a high maintenance sergeant; he needed constant and immediate attention.

Another night, he was again screaming for back up on the radio, again surrounded by Mexicans—this time in cars and trucks.

He demanded that every single unit drop what they were doing and come to his aid, so we hauled ass, what with it sounding like real danger.

Instead of finding him circled by gang bangers in some kind of combat formation, though, we found this: he'd pulled over a CB radio fan, part of a club of CBrs. Mostly misfits and bored white guys, they drove around all night and talked on their CBs to each other, playing a game they called "skunk."

Basically, it's Hide N' Seek in the city with cars, trucks, and CB radios: you describe where you are, and the rest of the group tries to find you.

Leeds had pulled over the Mexican-looking lead car that was hiding from the rest, then slowly, one-by-one, the other vehicles in the game had showed up at the scene with their engines idling and headlights on until about a dozen of them had Leeds surrounded and terrified.

We laughed—and hard—before getting around to explaining it to him.

He then said, "Fuck you" and drove off.

Who could believe that Leeds, a sergeant, didn't know about these guys?

I actually reported a lot of Leeds' little tics to prosecutors, then left it in their hands; I told them I couldn't be expected to testify, then work on the street with Leeds and his minions.

They said it was all kept confidential and that they'd go after him—but they never did.

A few days later, Leeds confronted me all by himself—and threatened to beat the shit out of me; he said he knew that I'd been to the prosecutors. He said that the "muscle stuff" with the Mexicans was to prove a point, to take a stand, and that if I didn't understand that then maybe I shouldn't be a cop.

Bullshit.

I told him he was out of control and had lost his perspective, which made it harder for the rest of us to do our jobs.

He disagreed and threatened again to beat hell out of me. I told him to bring it but that we both knew he was wrong. It was pretty heated.

Ultimately, he called me a pussy and stormed off, saying I should take a closer look at where I was headed.

What I learned from that little episode was that I couldn't trust the prosecutors. I was starting to feel really alone.

At one point a year or so later, Leeds actually stood up in front of briefing and apologized to the whole shift for the way he'd been acting the past few years, saying, "For a time, I lost my mind." He said he was better now and that he hoped we could all move on and work together.

This was a rare moment—but it only lasted for about a day; after that, Leeds found his mind again, so it didn't make that much of a difference in his behavior. It was most likely just a moment of supposed leadership, something the brass could check off.

I never taught at the police academy; I didn't think I'd be one of the guys they'd want the new recruits to meet. I was damaged and edgy, really fucked up, and I don't think they'd want the new people to see what the potential was in this job for totally messing with your head.

Leeds, however, would teach at the police academy.

Years later, when I was finally out of law enforcement, a young co-worker who was trying to get into police work excitedly began telling me about his academy classes when he found out I was an ex-cop.

He told me about one instructor whom I immediately recognized as Leeds. When I told him I knew Leeds, he began talking about the cases that Leeds would talk about, cases he handled both on patrol and as a detective, and how he learned over the years to talk to people to earn their trust.

I couldn't believe it; the bitch was recounting *my* cases as his cases. I guess night-sticking Mexicans didn't make it in to the curriculum.

I never did take the sergeant's exam.

I saw what they could become. There was something about getting anointed as an uber-cop and put in charge of others; maybe the extra spotlight, I don't know.

They start jostling for position to take the next step up, the next step away from being a real cop: making lieutenant.

Almost always, guys like Leeds got promoted to lieutenant. Don't even worry about it: placed in charge of an entire shift of officers—four, five, and six squads, plus sergeants—evaluating everyone's performance...I didn't want to be associated with those guys.

21 Not Knowing Your Place Means Life Or Death

ONE NIGHT, FOUR SEASONED GANGBANGERS were patrolling the main boulevard that marked the unofficial edge of wealthy suburbia. They were calm, looking for innocents to fuck with.

They were also too far above the part of town where gang members could walk at 2 a.m. without suspicion.

They'd hooted, luridly hissed, and made sexual remarks at a group of girls coming out of a convenience store. The girls then ran to their boyfriends and reported what had happened, and the boyfriends immediately went driving off in search of the bangers.

When they approached them, the gangbangers were still walking confidently along the boulevard.

Whatever the overconfident college boys said, it wasn't enough to intimidate the high school aged bangers, who startled them with their reaction: veterans of many gang fights, they spread out laterally as if they'd drilled for it, then approached in step—still calm—across the boulevard toward the college guys.

The largest of the four pulled out a knife; they were all gangbangers and young teens, but they were still gangsters, already veterans of the street, living up to an unwritten code.

It was the four suburban boyfriends in their early twenties who fled, piling back into their Volkswagen.

The large banger with the knife approached the driver's side window and flashed his knife inside, sinking it deep into the driver's chest.

The Volkswagen pulled forward, slowly at first, then lurched and bucked as the dying driver lost his life.

No one could remember a murder above the upscale foothill boulevard; "Probably never" was the general consensus.

Suddenly, though, the clean-living and wealthy were set upon by no doubt drug-addicted gang bangers who'd forgotten their place.

The incident got a lot of attention, and as Lead Detective, Skidmark had actually hustled his worthless ass and picked up three of the four assailants fairly quickly.

A couple months had passed, and Lt. Leeds was in his office, yelling at Skidmark. Both sworn enemies of mine, they were talking anxiously about Skidmark's idea for nabbing the fourth guy, the big guy who had the knife.

Leeds, Skidmark, and I had clashed regularly back when we were all in patrol.

Leeds had since been promoted from a sergeant to the lieutenant's spot and assigned to the Major Crimes Unit, which solved murders, and Skidmark was now one of his lead detectives.

I had been in the gang unit for a while, but even though this was a gang-involved crime, Major Crimes claimed it.

Skidmark's idea was actually a good one.

It was logical, it made sense, and it was painfully obvious: given the unit's expertise and regular dealings with these guys, he suggested coordinating with one of the gang detectives—in particular, he suggested me.

The gang unit had been a joke when it first formed up, not acting much differently than any other patrol squad.

A few of us, though, had transformed it with a different approach: instead of trying to beat hell out of every gangbanger we identified, we built a database, organized the names by groups, and got to know them by developing intelligence files.

We were exploring new ground by utilizing the tendency of rival gangs to quietly rat each other out to police when motivated and given the opportunity.

No one was supposed to talk to us, but they all did, and we'd collected thousands of names.

Skidmark told Leeds that he'd talked to everyone he knew, asking them all for help.

He'd also interrogated the hell out of every gangster in the city, but he couldn't find the last guy involved in the murder, the one who was the actual killer and had the most to lose. He'd gone deep.

I'd just dropped by the detective division to talk to the few people I still got along with and was just leaving as I passed Leeds' door and caught wind of what the two of them were talking about.

"You know I don't want to ask him for help, but if we're gonna get this last guy, we have to try."

"I don't fucking like this; you know what I think of that guy," Leeds growled. "He's not a team player. He's not...well, you know how he is. You of all people know. He's not one of us; not one of us at all. If you get any information from him, you keep it quiet. We can solve our own cases. This is bullshit. He won't find him anyway, and if he does you don't tell anyone he helped you. Do you understand me?"

He was yelling at that point, telling Skidmark to go ahead with his idea.

Leaning against the wall a few feet down the hall from Leeds' office, I was smiling when Skidmark came out; when he saw me, his shoulders dropped.

With all that I'd just heard, I couldn't help thinking of that line from an old zombie horror movie. I forget the name, but the zombies were prone to chanting in unison, "One of us...one of us..."

Skidmark called me at home that night.

He said he knew I'd overheard the conversation in Leeds' office, and he needed my help.

He then told me what he knew about the fourth man, specifically which gang he belonged to and the guy's nickname, "Joker."

"Do you know him?" he asked.

"Of course, I fucking know him," I said. *Don't insult me; I've already reached my limit with you.*

Then he asked me to give him information on my informants.

I laughed. There was no way that was going to happen.

It didn't immediately occur to me that I might have to explain the whole concept of confidentiality to Skidmark; nevertheless, I said I had an understanding with my informants and that I never disclosed who gave me information—no matter what.

A gangster's own homeboys would beat his ass if they knew he even *looked* at a police officer—so if the rival gang got wind of him providing intelligence, he was dead.

I made it clear that no one—not Skidmark, Leeds, the Chief—no one would ever get that information, *ever.*

After a long pause, he said, "OK."

I told him if he wanted my help, I'd ask around, and if I got any information on Joker I'd call him. For his part, he had to guarantee that no matter what time of day or night I called, he would come; if he couldn't make that promise, then I wouldn't help him. He agreed.

He then said that he could pay my informants if they produced. I told him they all worked for free, but if he wanted to give me money to pass along I'd do it after the fact. He wasn't comfortable with this, but he agreed. He wanted control; too fucking bad.

I called an informant who I knew would know about Joker's gang and asked where he'd been and if he was still in the city. The guy asked why I wanted to know.

He hadn't heard, so I filled him in on the details of the murder— quick to add that the police department's finest couldn't locate Joker anywhere and "needed the help of two fucked up, wannabe thugs like us to get this dude." I knew he'd like that. He laughed, and we exchanged insults on which of us really was the wannabe.

I knew he'd ask around and see what he could find out. He loved this shit, acting like an undercover cop; he was thrilled by the chance to make a difference in his town and outperform some of the more abusive cops when it came to hunting down bad guys.

He didn't like Leeds or Skidmark, and he knew Joker had fucked up.

I told him to call anytime, day or night (our standard practice). He knew I'd never give him up; when I asked for a favor, it was always big.

Two days later, at 10:30 p.m., I got the call.

Joker was at an apartment building in the inner city just a block up from Main Street, one of those apartments clustered for partying and affordable housing for parolees, gangbangers, and shitbags of the night. I got the address and called Skidmark.

He was reluctant. It was late, and he was tired.

I unloaded. "Look, motherfucker, if you want this dude, he's there now. I'm on my way, and this isn't even my fucking case. Get off your fucking ass and get in here, or I'll arrest him myself and let Leeds know you had a shot and didn't take it."

After hearing that, Skidmark said he was on his way.

When he arrived, we coordinated deployment.

He wanted the front, and I was supposed to go around to the back.

In typical Skidmark standard operating procedure, he was trying to bully his way in the front door with a patrol unit behind him.

We were working without warrants, and he needed to apply some finesse—but he didn't have any.

I was in the back, listening to his bullshit game and thinking to myself that some people will never learn.

Suddenly, the back door opened—and there was Joker.

He stepped out of the apartment and slowly walked down the stairs, all stealth and silent. Hidden in the shadows with my gun pointed at his head, I spoke up.

"'Sup, Joker."

He turned to me and said, "'Sup Pacman."

Another one of my nicknames.

"Not a thing," I said. "Just out to get some air."

"Ya, it's nice out tonight."

"So, what's it gonna be? You tired of running? We gonna fight, or do we do this like men?"

"Ya, I'm tired of running."

I had him turn around, then I cuffed him.

No disrespect; it was over.

I told him, "Skidmark is up front, and you gave him a run for his money. In the end, the motherfucker had to come to me to find you, so you keep your head up. You didn't go down like a bitch, alright?"

"Thanks, man," he said.

We went to the front of the apartment where Skidmark was still trying to bully his way in, and I handed Joker over to him.

He said thanks to me, then immediately started in on Joker about what a piece of shit he was.

I went home and called my informant. He had a perfect record for finds and information, and I gave him the play-by-play on what had happened. I also mentioned that he might get some money this time and asked if he was interested. He said that he was, so I passed a couple hundred bucks along to him.

For some time after that, I thought I might have to testify. To make matters worse, Leeds and Skidmark wouldn't even look at me if we passed in the hallway.

Joker's family hired a lawyer who played the media like a flute, promising to bring Joker's twisted background out at trial. He was underprivileged, unemployed, and even likely had brain damage from early drug use and unhealthy gang influences...Christ, he was only seventeen.

When the family ran out of money, the attorney just pled him in. Didn't even bring any of that stupid shit up at sentencing; just pled him in. Just the lawyer's standard "I'll submit it, Your Honor" when the judge asked if the defense had any statement to assist the court.

The fact that I was the officer who found and arrested Joker for murder was never made public.

22 Listening...A Lost Art

WORKING THE WORST AREA OF the largest city has had effects on me that I'm still just finding out about.

One day I was on the street, talking with a woman from central city, the oldest part of town with the lowest rents and highest number of parolees, ex-cons, and mental subjects.

She said that the residents saw us as too afraid to get out of our patrol cars, afraid to get out and face what the city had become. We didn't walk it, live it, and breathe it like they did.

I thought she was joking, messing with me maybe.

I left the call I was on and thought about it as I drove around in the car and listened to the radio.

I watched the people as I passed by, hearing dispatch describe the usual horrific details of life in the boiled-down, foreign language of the 10-code.

I stopped and talked to an older guy I knew who'd lived in the area a long time, asking him what he thought. Did people see us as afraid?

"Yep," he said. "You guys do seem afraid, driving around, never getting out of your cars, never talking to folks, yep, it does look that way."

I made up my mind then and there that I'd get out and walk as much as I could. Never again would I leave a call to do paperwork and not return.

I made it a point to write my paperwork at the scene and get out of the car on slow nights or early in the morning and walk, look around, and listen.

The world was different on foot; screams, gunshots, and blood trails appeared out of nowhere on the sidewalk, then disappeared just as well. The whole feel of the city was different on foot.

As a field-training officer, I made my trainees get out as well.

There was one guy that I really liked; we hit it off immediately. He was quiet, thoughtful, and listened to people—and yet he could be hard and tough as nails; one didn't cancel out the other.

Working the central city one quiet Friday morning, maybe 3 a.m., I pulled over and told him to get out and walk.

At first, he looked at me like I was crazy and just shook his head no. Then I shut off the engine and got out, and he followed.

I said, "I mean it; we're gonna walk."

He rolled his eyes but walked beside me.

I told him the story of the woman and what she'd said to me, as well as the old man's comments. I then told him that I never felt afraid but that if people thought we were afraid, we'd lost their respect.

The further away from the car we walked, the more jumpy he became, looking behind us as we walked. Every scream and gunshot made him hop, but I just kept walking and talking to him.

When we were several blocks from the car, I stopped and turned to him and said, "You're afraid, aren't you?"

He said he felt vulnerable; he was away from the car, which was his security with its mobility and communication. He felt safer by the car.

"Look at it from their point of view, the people we work for, the people who live here," I said. "You've got forty-five rounds of ammo, a bulletproof vest, a night stick, pepper spray, and training. You get on the radio, and you have back up in seconds. Is that right?"

"Sure," he said.

I continued, "What do they have? The women, kids, and old people who live in this area? They have nothing like that. They have you and me. They depend on us to be there for them."

He got a strange look on his face; I could see that I'd reached him.

"You may be afraid, but you have to walk this area, any area you get. You can't let your fear make *them* live in fear. Get out and walk and listen to your area. Listen for how it's supposed to sound, and when it doesn't, talk to people. See what's going on in the neighborhoods you patrol."

I can get preachy like that, rambling sometimes, so just to lighten the message I added, "Don't feel like you have to put your ear to the sidewalk. Listening is just a big part of this job; it can make it much easier."

We started to walk again. Still visibly nervous, he was much more relaxed at that point, understanding that he was setting an example.

A block later, we came across a huge pool of blood.

It was relatively fresh on the sidewalk, and a trail led away from it. It didn't really go anywhere, eventually disappearing in the grass of a vacant lot.

"You see, this is what the people on the street see, what they live in. We never would have found this if we hadn't gotten out and walked."

We never did find out what the pool of blood was about or who its owner was.

I checked the area, then the local hospitals, but no one had come in either injured, stabbed, or shot. Whoever it was had lost a lot of blood; nevertheless, I'd impacted my trainee.

After he was out on his own, complete with a patrol car and bloody streets to monitor, I heard him frequently sign out in his area and go it on foot. I don't know if anyone else thought it mattered or not, but it did to me.

You can't expect people to walk the streets if armed Cops won't.

Later, while working in central city again (as was usual those days), I had another trainee with me.

His name was Jeff McKell, and he was actually a reservist, not yet a certified peace officer hired and sworn. He asked to ride with me, and after a few hours he said to me, "You don't work like anyone else I've ridden with."

We heard a call come over about a large male breaking into an apartment a few blocks away. He'd beaten the occupants pretty badly, then left on foot, running.

Manu Rio had been active in the street gangs there, but he'd left town a few years earlier when his gang had fallen apart, taken over by a rival gang. Rio had a girl in the city and had missed her a lot. Finally, he had enough and came back to visit, riding the bus from several states over.

When he got there, there she was in her apartment—having sex with some other dude.

He was devastated.

He kicked the guy's ass and beat her up pretty badly, and we came across him on foot some four blocks west of the chaos he'd just left behind.

Manu was a huge man, maybe 6-foot-4, and he was built like a linebacker and mean as hell. He had a reputation on the street as a brawler, particularly a guy who liked to fight cops.

I got out and approached him—and he squared off with me right away, assuming a fighting stance; he was covered with sweat, all warmed up and ready to go.

I could see that he was exhausted and visibly devastated, so I started to try to talk him down; it was obvious that he didn't want to fight if he didn't have to.

I started to talk to him quietly, then just listened to get him talking.

He told me about his girl and the long drive he'd just made, thinking about how much he missed her. They had a baby together, and he wanted to be a man and be the baby's father. He went on and on, getting everything off his chest.

He was emotionally wounded and upset, so I just listened to him and let him vent.

When he looked like he was about done, I let the other cars know that I had him and gave them our location.

They lit up lights and sirens, and we could hear them coming.

I told Manu that he had a choice to make, that I wanted to help him and understood what he was going through, but I also needed him to trust me.

Naturally, he was suspicious; he's a banger, and I'm a cop. I told him, though, that with all the other units coming I had a minimal amount of time to get him safely into my car; I didn't want to see him hurt, but the reality was that we had a lot of new guys who were hotheaded and looking to make a name for themselves.

On top of that, they'd heard of him and his attitude toward cops. So, I asked him again to trust me and let me take him into custody before the other guys showed up.

As the sirens closed in, he stood his ground and said, "Fuck it. I wanna fight them bitches."

"Look man," I said, "Let's resolve this like men. You don't have to prove shit to anyone. I'll even give you the cuffs, and you can put them on and get into my car."

As I handed him my cuffs, McKell's eyes were huge and his mouth dropped open. I had nothing to lose. If he listened and cuffed himself, I didn't have to fight him and he'd be in my car when the backup arrived; if he didn't, we'd be fighting—but I'd have a lot of help in the next few moments.

He stared at me for a few seconds, holding the cuffs and listening to the sirens getting closer. Finally, he said "OK" and cuffed himself. I opened the door, and he got into the car. Then I seat-belted him in and closed the door as the first unit arrived, officers jumping from the car with their nightsticks out. They wanted to know where Manu was. Did he already run off?

I said, "No, he's here," and explained that I'd asked him politely to cuff himself and get into my car—and he had. As proof, I pointed to him sitting in my patrol car.

"Bullshit!" they exclaimed. "You did *not* get Manu Rio in your car without a fight."

I said, "OK, if you say so," then got in the car as more units arrived.

While I spoke to Manu, taking down his information for my report, they all stood outside the car, nightsticks quivering, glaring like I was the high school principal who'd canceled the rumble after a big game.

They asked McKell if what I said had actually happened.

"Ya, I wouldn't have believed it if I hadn't seen it," he said.

I was pretty proud of that moment.

I thought of it as an accomplishment—and I'd certainly disappointed a lot of my co-workers.

Listening wasn't rocket science; it was just common sense.

23 Bad Stop Ben

ONCE I HAD A NEW guy, Ben, develop a really interesting habit of stopping cars.

He had no legal reason to stop and search them with no probable cause, which was the lowest legal standard of evidence on which we were allowed to act.

It's a fairly simple concept, really: "probable" as in it probably could be suspicious to a reasonable person.

He made a lot of arrests with this "style" of his, but they wouldn't stick; prosecutors wouldn't file charges on them, and any defense attorney worth his pay could get them thrown out.

One night, I was called to back up Ben, "back" as we called it; it happened a lot that he always needed a back.

He was at the south end on one of the main streets of the city, which wasn't a cop-friendly area. He'd stopped a truck that had left a suspected drug house. We'd do it if we could—but we can't, so we don't.

Pulling over everyone who departs a suspicious house not only wastes a lot of time, but it can get a department sued more than it needs to be. Besides, "suspected drug house" just isn't enough to go on.

Probable cause is also the standard for a warrant to shut down a drug house, and if we had it we'd close the place.

Anyway, Ben had the suspected drug house customers pulled over and asked me to standby while he talked to the three people in the truck.

He asked the driver if he could search the truck; the driver consented. Ben searched the truck and found nothing.

He then searched the passengers, and one had a purse with drugs inside. He arrested all the occupants and impounded the truck.

I knew the search was bad and that the arrests wouldn't hold up, and I tried to explain it to Ben—but he wouldn't listen.

Trying for common sense, I told him to take the drugs, flush them somewhere, and send them on their way. Ben wouldn't budge.

About a week later, he got a letter from the prosecutors telling him that the search was illegal and that the arrests had been thrown out and squashed.

This went on for months: Ben stopping people, illegal searches, arrests being tossed.

Another night, he pulled over a car because "it was a car full of Mexicans driving around at four in the morning."

I couldn't believe he said it out loud. He had all the occupants out sitting on the curb in handcuffs.

Several other cars had rolled up, as well as a Sergeant, and Ben started to search the car when he got permission from the non-English speaking driver who agreed with whatever Ben said to him.

The trunk was full of used car stereos, and Ben and the Sergeant decided that the property was obviously stolen, so they arrested everybody. We, the rest of the squad, about shit ourselves at this brilliance.

The stop was bad—which made the search illegal—and the property hadn't been proven to be stolen. The people hadn't even been checked for warrants yet, but they were checked later—and they would all have none.

We all left, driving off and refusing to come back.

Ben and the Sergeant dealt with all the paperwork: the impounding of the illegally stopped vehicle, property forms for the illegally seized stereos, and booking of the illegally arrested Mexicans.

The next day, we had a heated debate with the Sergeant in shift briefing.

He said he never wanted to see that lack of teamwork again, but we pushed back, bringing the Constitution into the discussion, as well as the Fourth Amendment, search and seizure rights, oaths, and our assertion that this stop was bad from jump.

Regardless, this went on and on.

The Chief and Assistant Chiefs came in one day and awarded Ben "Officer of the Year" for all of his felony arrests, then sat in the shift briefing and told each of us that we needed to learn from his example. He had twice as many arrests and seized more property than any of us "and he's new."

You could almost hear our respect for the brass evaporate from the room.

Ben lost almost every case he made an arrest on, but the department didn't track convictions. This got to be a joke on patrol: just go out and be an idiot, and management will reward you.

It didn't really stop until Ben caught his wife with another man and planned to kill her—but passed out drunk in the midst of the attempt.

He'd left a murder/suicide note, and she found it and called the police.

Ben was arrested and ultimately lost his police certification over it. Years later, he and I became friends; he was a good guy when he was sober and not asked to be a cop.

Grecko Wrestling 24

ROBERT ALLEN WAS A MEAN schizophrenic, and he could have easily taken on both Manu and Doobie.

He lived in some mid-block apartment in the central city and suddenly got very loud and violent for no apparent reason but his illness. I got a call to his apartment from his neighbors.

He was enormous, almost 6-and-a-half feet tall and 300 pounds or more, depending on his condition at the time. His weight could vary a lot.

When I got the call, dispatch told me that Allen's address had been flagged as the occupant being very dangerous and prone to fighting cops in the nude for fun.

They sent me a back-up as well; the back that night was Skidmark—and with no **Street Creds** or common sense, he'd get both our asses kicked by Allen, so I canceled his ass and went in alone.

I knocked on the door for several minutes, listening to Allen yelling inside as he carried on a conversation with—it later turned out—himself.

He finally answered the door, totally naked, yelling and screaming at me, "What the fuck do you want? What son of a bitch has called you to my house?"

Dispatch then informed me that Allen did have a warrant, and that made the call a lot more interesting; now, I was required to arrest him since I'd found him there at the house.

I talked to Allen for some time, with dispatch checking on me frequently; they were nervous.

The last group of cops who had come there had battled with Allen, and he'd fucked them up pretty bad. Dispatch had pulled the case and read it: the cops had been some guys considered heavyweights in the department, guys who were known for being able to handle themselves on the street—and Allen had beaten the hell out of them.

So, Allen was well known to the force.

He had a habit of talking to you one minute—then in the next, in mid-sentence, changing his manner and growling or barking or charging at you, trying to start a fight.

I didn't respond to his aggression; instead, I just kept talking to him.

He finally asked me, "What are you planning on doing, officer? Are you gonna arrest me or what?"

I told him that I was going to arrest him and that he had a choice as to how that was going to happen.

I told him that he had quite a reputation for fighting and that he'd harmed some of the officers who arrested him the last time.

I said that I could tell he wasn't the kind of guy that he acted like he was and that I was going to give him the chance to prove it. I'd come alone, and we could either walk out like men or fight; the choice was his.

Just then, Chad Stiver showed up. He was a guy I trusted. He wasn't well liked in the department either, but we'd clicked.

He sat back and listened to me deal with Allen. Dispatch had called him, worried about Allen going off. He knew about Allen and his history, but he didn't interfere with how I was handling him.

When Allen saw Stiver, he did go off, flying into a rage. I calmed him back down, though, after he charged me multiple times, still naked and mad as hell.

I explained that Stiver was there because of the previous time that we'd shown up and he'd beaten up a couple cops. He wasn't there to fight; instead, he'd shown up to see if Allen was going to go willingly this time, not fighting like a crazy man.

He got angry about this, yelling, "I *am* fucking crazy! I *am* fucking crazy, and you know that!"

I had to think quickly; he was escalating, breathing hard and sweating, getting amped up for a fight.

So, talking more and more quietly as he became increasingly angry, I said, "You may be crazy, Robert; I don't know. I don't care about that. I've been honest with you and told you that I have to arrest you. I've treated you with respect, and I hope that I've earned your respect. Now get your clothes on, and let's go to the jail. I'll walk you out so that all your neighbors can see that you aren't a bad man and they shouldn't be afraid of you."

He watched me for a few minutes, panting and glaring; I stared back, not saying a word.

Then, in a split second he said, "OK I'll go if you promise not to beat me up like last time."

I did promise, and so did Stiver.

Allen got dressed and allowed me to handcuff him. I then walked him to my car, and we laughed and joked along the way, his neighbors watching our every move; they were terrified of him.

He was booked into jail without incident.

The next day in the shift briefing, Stiver told everyone that he saw something last night that he'd never seen before. "Slick talked Robert Allen into walking to his car without a fight. Allen is one of the most dangerous people in the whole fucking city, and he had him eating out of his hand."

He looked at the sergeant and said, "This is the kind of shit we should be recognizing instead of bullshit bad arrests and ass kissers."

They glared at each other for a while, and the room was quiet. Stiver had a way of making friends with the brass like I did.

I had a lot of experience with mentally ill people. Central city is stuffed full of them. Halfway houses, people living on Social Security for mental problems, lesbians, gays—not saying they're mental, but the ones who end up in central city have a lot of issues, such as sexual abuse, poor coping skills, and the inability to attach in a healthy relationship.

Seriously, we used to refer to central city as the dumping ground of the broken and damaged.

I learned a lot from working the area day after day.

Allen could have ripped me apart if he wanted, but I sensed something in him "like a dog that barks too much." The real killers are quiet and might growl before they strike. They don't bark to warn you; he did.

All of this made me suspect with the rest of the force. I was criticized for going in to too many calls without back. I did that, though, so I'd have a chance to talk and listen.

There were too many guys who would cowboy in and make the situation worse with the tough guy bullshit; I'd cancel back-up once I heard who the officer would be, not because of the call.

Fighting wasn't a victory for me.

I don't like how it makes me feel; I feel like a failure when I fight because it means that I misjudged the situation. I believe I should be able to think my way out of anything, and most times I did.

Most cops see things from the perspective of being in control; I don't see that at all. As cops, I never think that we're in control of anything, so I don't try to be. It's a fallacy.

I let the scene unfold, the interviews unfold, the cases unfold. I don't force it.

I was never afraid of not rising to the occasion. My fear was that when it was over, I'd have reacted too quickly, too harshly, and not be able to live with it.

Giving Victims A Bad Name

ONE NIGHT, I WAS DISPATCHED to this formerly very exclusive club in town; it was one of those places that for so long had been a men-only club, then a membership joint for the high rollers who could afford it.

It was old school and old money but was so far out of step with reality that it finally closed altogether and is now either a wedding reception parlor or a bingo club. I forget which.

This night, one of the waitresses was missing; the manager said that the girl had just disappeared in the middle of her shift, and he was worried that she'd been abducted—or worse. The waitress was extremely dependable, so he was convinced that something bad had happened.

I called in other units, and we checked the club and the parking lot for any signs of the young missing waitress. She'd left her purse behind, but nothing else.

Apparently, no one had seen her leave. The people at the tables she'd been serving said that one minute she was there, and the next she was gone.

The bar patrons were a surprisingly uncooperative bunch. We were rarely summoned there.

When I was in vice, I heard rumors of college girls making large sums of money for having sex with businessmen there; however, I could never prove it.

I did interview one girl who told me about dating "Q-tips"; that was her term for older gray or white-haired men. She said that the Q-tips would have a lot of money and were more mature than younger men. She felt that they'd have better places to take a girl who was willing to be entertained. She denied having sex with any of the Q-tips for money, but she said that if they left her a gift after sex, she wouldn't refuse it. She was only twenty years old.

Anyway, we searched for signs of the missing waitress with only the abandoned purse to go on. I put out a BOLO ("Be On the Look Out") for her and cleared the club.

Checking her apartment turned up nothing. I stopped to write up the case, and when I was almost done a call came in reporting a woman who had turned up at some guy's door, claiming to have been raped. It was the missing waitress.

Our victim said she'd been abducted from the club by a group of men, then driven around the city in a car while they took turns raping her. When they were done, she said they dumped her off and she went to the nearest house for help.

I interviewed her as she was attended to by medical, then followed as she was transported to the hospital, speaking to her in the Emergency Room.

She claimed that she'd been serving a table of professional men at the club who had been making suggestive remarks to her all night; she hadn't responded to them, instead remaining polite in her refusals.

Finally, they'd left, and she went on break for a minute, when she saw one of them in the parking lot alone; she said that he "looked sad," so she went over to see what was wrong.

She said he then hit her on the head and knocked her out.

When she came to, she was in the back of a vehicle with many men in the car who took turns raping her, cheering each other on.

I did see that her clothes were torn and that she had some mud on her arms and face. Her hair was also messy, but something about her demeanor wasn't right.

Her blouse had all the buttons, and her socks were clean—as were her shoes—and she showed no signs of physical violence; she just looked disheveled. Her eye contact was really good as well.

She was sitting on a gurney in her black and white waitress outfit while we talked.

Her manner and behavior changed as I questioned her: she started biting her lip, and she made suggestive eye contact as she started flirting with me. I was surprised, but I didn't respond; instead, I waited to see how this would unfold.

Finally, she ran her hand up the inside of her legs and slowly opened them while looking away; she was making sure that I looked at her crotch, her legs spread there on the gurney in the ER as we discussed her gang rape; I did look, and I noticed that she still had her panties on. They were white cotton panties with no blood, no dirt—and they weren't even semen-stained.

As we kept talking, I noticed that her eyes were more dilated than they should have been in the well-lit room. So, I asked her if she'd been drinking, and she said that she hadn't and that it wasn't allowed on the job.

She sat for the Perk kit test, as they call it, to check for fluids in her vaginal tract.

The doctor later said that there was no evidence collected; there was nothing there, no semen, no hair, and no sign that she'd had sex recently.

Checking with the ER nurse, I was told that every patient who gets a blood draw has an alcohol screen done as well. Her blood alcohol level was at .17—more than twice the legal limit.

I told the victim that I was going to go out and look for the men who had raped her; instead, I went back to the club.

I kept asking around until I finally found a waitress who would talk to me. She said that the victim had been flirting with a table of guys and that she'd observed her sneaking a drink with them as the night progressed. The guys had asked her to leave with them, and she told the other waitress that she was leaving with them and to "fuck this shitty job" as she was "going to party."

I wrote up my report and forwarded it to detectives.

I then went to our victim's apartment to tell her that the detectives would contact her in the morning. I found her there, drinking beer with a group of guys and listening to music—and she was the only woman in the apartment.

She claimed that I didn't care about her and said that all cops were worthless and that I could just go to hell! She then went back to partying.

The detective did contact her, and she eventually admitted that she hadn't been raped and had made up the whole story to try to keep her job; she said that she'd gotten drunk at work and left and that this was all she could think of to avoid getting fired.

We made sure that this was unofficially relayed to the club—and she was then fired.

Blood Bath 26

I WAS PARKED IN THE early morning hours, talking to dispatch on a pay phone in a downtown parking lot.

It was located near an old medical building, one of those pay phones you could pull up to and drive right alongside and dial without leaving your car.

I used it as often as possible because drug dealers also liked it; it makes them pissed to see a fully equipped, decked-out police cruiser with all the decals and electronics parked at their work phone.

I can't go up to a drug dealer and tell him to get off the phone—not legally, at least—but I can totally fuck up his day using that same phone myself, answering it when it rings and wrecking his **Street Creds.**

"Police department, can I help you?" The line goes dead; another satisfied customer. The little things make me smile.

That night, I was getting the details on a case that I was working, when around the corner of the building about thirty yards away came a woman stumbling across the parking lot.

It was dark, and there were no lights, so she looked to me like a transient, a drunk one.

Her hair was a mess, and I could see that her clothes were filthy as well. I thought she was probably going to stumble up to me to try to ask for money or a ride somewhere, and I didn't want to be bothered with some nasty ass, panhandling, alcohol—soaked transient needing a favor.

I couldn't tell if she'd seen me yet, as I was parked in the dark, talking on the phone, so I waited for her to get closer; sure enough, I could see that she truly was a mess, hair all screwed up like her clothes—and in the early morning light it looked like she'd pissed her pants.

I hung up the phone, cursing, and turned on my headlights and spotlight at the same time to encourage her, hopefully, just to go away.

The picture in my mind of what this woman would look like—leaves in her hair, missing teeth, urine-stained clothes, and more than likely vomit on her shirt and pants—was instantly transformed. She was lit up, night became day, and it took a moment for the real image to sink in.

She was a 16-year-old girl, stumbling across the parking lot. She was in shock—not drunk—and she was covered in blood from head to toe.

The hair that I assumed would be filled with leaves and lice was instead caked in blood clots; it stuck out in different directions, stiffened from dried blood. Her face was streaked with blood, and her clothes torn and covered in blood.

What I assumed would be urine stains on her pants was actually blood shining in the light, dark red and fresh. She looked like she'd just walked out of a horror movie; picture the original "Carrie" by Stephen King with Sissy Spacek in the prom bloodbath, and you get the idea.

I'd never seen anyone alive and covered in this much blood—much less walking.

She didn't react to my spotlight or headlights and just kept walking towards me, eyes staring straight ahead.

I drove toward her and got out of the car. I was sure that she'd been in a bad car accident and had somehow walked this far; there was just too much blood for it to be anything else.

I asked her what happened, and she stared at me, registering for the first time that she was somewhere else. She blinked, mouth open, eyes blank, and mouthing words—but no sound came out. She finally said, "My boyfriend raped me."

At first, I didn't believe her. There was way too much blood to be from one person, much less from a rape. She started to faint, and I grabbed her.

She told me, "I want to see my mommy."

"Mommy.".. just like that...said it like the child she used to be.

I told her I had to call the paramedics and that we'd see her mom as soon as we could, but the paramedics had to come first.

She started getting hysterical, crying that she "wanted her mommy."

I finally had to say, "OK, OK. We'll do that right now. You'll have to get into my car, and we'll go find her. Can you remember where you live?"

She said yes.

I got an old army blanket for her from the trunk of my car, helped her get in, then seat-belted her. She stared out the window, just blank, oblivious...no emotion.

I asked her who her boyfriend was, and she calmly gave me a name: Robert Harris, Jr. She said that they'd agreed to meet that night at his house to have sex. They'd been dating only a short while and hadn't had sex yet, so tonight was going to be the first time.

When she got to his place, things immediately went to shit.

First, he demanded a blowjob—and when she refused, it got ugly. He pulled out a knife and began cutting her repeatedly, she said, anally and vaginally. Then he smeared the blood on her face and hair. It all happened in his room in the basement of the house.

I asked her to show me where he lived, which was only a block from where we'd run into each other.

She said she'd waited a very long time for him to fall asleep, then fled.

We pulled up in front of the house, and I stopped.

Was he alone in the house? She thought so.

I sat there, thinking. I wanted to go in and put a bullet in his head, seriously mulling this over. I imagined walking in to his room, with him asleep on a bloodstained bed—and I'd add his brains to the mess.

I gripped the steering wheel tighter and started breathing hard. In the straining silence, the girl finally spoke again, asking, "You're not gonna go in there, are you?"

I told her I was thinking about it, that he deserved to die. Then I asked her, "What do you want me to do?"

"Mommy," she replied.

Suddenly, I was struck by how stupid I was handling this.

I had to take care of her first; that was the main priority. I wanted him dead—no doubt—but I didn't have that luxury now. I had to get her to her mother without her going into shock, then to the nearest hospital.

I was shaking with rage—actually seeing red like I was looking through a camera lens with a red filter—but I drove away on to her mother's house; necessity had just saved Robert, Jr.'s life.

I told the girl to stay in the car while I went to the front door for her mom.

After several knocks, she finally answered, and I informed her that I needed her to come with her daughter and me to the hospital right away.

She started yelling and screaming, "I'm sick of that fucking kid. All she ever does is cause problems. You can take her to jail and throw away the keys. I don't fucking care."

Then she started down the front porch steps to go chew her daughter out, the "no good piece of shit."

I grabbed her by the shirt and slammed her against the post of the porch. Then, talking quietly right in her face, I said, "Listen, you stupid bitch. Your daughter is seriously fucking hurt, bleeding, and in shock. I need to get her to the hospital, but she demanded that I bring her to you first. She said that she wanted 'her mommy.'

"You are going to get in the car and for once in your fucked up life be a parent. You say one word, anything that's less than kind, and I will personally beat your fucking ass."

I was in no mood for this dysfunctional shit.

I asked her, "You got that?" Startled at that point, and a bit frightened, she said that she did.

I walked her to the car and put her in the back seat, then told the girl her mom was there and that we were going to the hospital. She reached over to the back seat for her mother, who held her hand, then closed her eyes and was much calmer, her breathing beginning to slow down. Her mom looked at me with real fear. I don't know if she was afraid of me or afraid for her daughter, but she was very quiet in the back seat, staring at me.

Meanwhile, we were on our way to the closest hospital. I called ahead and said that we were en route to the ER and that I needed them to have a wheelchair ready and waiting outside the door.

I was in the ER often because of the area I worked (the inner city), so they knew me. The nurse I spoke to was a friend and asked what I was bringing them. As code, I told her that she'd need a PERK kit; that's the medical kit they use to do a rape exam in order to collect semen or other evidence.

She said, "OK. Is it bad?"

I said "Yes, very."

We pulled into the ER parking lot, and they had the chair waiting. When they saw the girl, they had the same reaction that I did: total shock.

They carefully helped her out of the car and immediately took her to a room.

While they did the exam, I called for a detective. One showed up a short time later, coming in with the typical casual attitude.

He said, "So is this the usual 'I got caught by my parents having sex and now it's rape?'"

I said no, then explained the case, emphasizing how bad it was—and his demeanor changed instantly.

"Let's go talk to her," he said.

We looked into the room she was in, and CSI was taking pictures of the bloody handprints on her back, chest, and legs. She was sitting on a gurney, still bleeding on the white sheets, and she turned to us and looked at the detective, her hair still matted with blood.

She turned away, ashamed, and a doctor told us to leave, which we did.

The detective was visibly shaken, even with his seventeen years or so of experience on the force.

"Is all that blood hers?"

I said that it was. I told him what had happened and told him about Robert, Jr. He said he would take care of it.

I finished my report at the hospital and left the case for him to finish.

The doctor told me it was the worst case of rape that he'd seen in over twenty-five years as an ER doctor. They had her into surgery for all the internal damage, and he didn't know if she'd be able to have children. He was pretty angry when we spoke.

"I hope you find this piece of shit and give him some of that street justice you guys talk about."

I was really surprised by this. Usually, doctors weren't real fond of our stories of scuffles and battles; since they had to clean up our mess, they weren't happy about it.

The girl eventually recovered, and Robert, Jr. was caught.

He fled the state first, though, and the FBI eventually picked him up after his family, mother, and sister turned him in for the reward money.

When we went to court, his attorney was one of the veterans; gruff, overbearing, and skilled at intimidating cops into making mistakes on the stand.

At the preliminary hearing, a mini-trial meant to get a judge's blessing that at least enough evidence existed to advance a case to trial, he asked to speak to me before the hearing.

The victim couldn't remember much of what had happened, and he wanted to know what I would testify to about the "alleged rape." ..he framed it that way: "alleged."

I noted what his "alleged client" had done and what the girl had looked like stumbling up to me, blood-soaked, in the parking lot. "Please do take this to a jury," I said. "I would love to explain this to them."

He looked me in the eye as I spoke, measuring how I'd come across on the stand, then said, "OK, we're through" and walked away to meet with his client in another room.

After a while, he came out and in open court told the judge that Robert, Jr., was going to plead guilty straight up to all four counts of aggravated sexual assault against him, five-to-life coming with each one.

He claimed that he was on meth that night and didn't remember much; at least that was his story. He remembered enough to run to California for six months before his own family turned him in.

I would love to be able to erase that night with her in the parking lot.

Years later, during my divorce, my ex-wife would run into the mom who I'd threatened that night. She asked my ex if she was married to the cop she knew who did so much for her daughter. She told her story about that night and asked her to thank me for what I'd done.

The ex—one of many—called me and told me of the encounter. "Why didn't you ever tell me this story?"

I answered that she never wanted to talk about my work and wouldn't have listened.

"Well, I guess you finally did at least one thing that was good," she said.

There was a reason we were getting a divorce.

27 Stupid Is As Stupid Does

I GUESS IT'S OBVIOUS BY now that I don't often see people at their best on this job. It makes cops suspicious, wary of pretty much everybody—all of you, even your beliefs.

The notion of a God, a higher power, even the idea that some kind of order exists in the universe, is victimized on a regular basis on police calls.

We've got to cope somehow, and sometimes it's in a sick way. It's just comical, and the laughs can come perfectly timed to ease the load of pondering all the serious dysfunction we have to walk through.

One night, I was dispatched to the parking lot of the ER at a hospital.

A night clerk had gone out to her car and unlocked the doors. She had a lot of personal items to load into the back seat, and she set her keys on the hood of the car while she did so. Then, she got into the car and locked the doors because she was afraid of getting carjacked or attacked.

She looked all over the car for her keys, going through her pockets, her purse, and all the stuff on the back seat, but she couldn't find them.

She sat there a while, trying to remember where they were. Then it finally came to her: they were on the hood of the car right in front of her. Panicked, she started to cry, then called 911.

She told the dispatcher what had happened, the nature of her plight, and that she was locked in her car. Dispatch had sent me to make sure that this wasn't some kind of distress code; they wanted me to ensure that nothing else was wrong because it was simply unbelievable that someone could be this dumb.

I could picture the scene in dispatch, with the other dispatchers gathering around to listen to this drama unfolding.

Since all 911 calls are recorded, their professionalism this time came down to keeping a straight face.

Many questions would have to remain unanswered: how did this woman ever score a driver license? Is she allowed to vote? Are there children involved? Has she reproduced? They couldn't believe she was for real, as several minutes were needed to calm her down.

"Push the unlock button on the driver's side door," the dispatcher instructed calmly.

The woman did this, and magically the car unlocked.

She was so relieved, no longer imprisoned and needing someone or a locksmith to get the keys off the hood to open the door, or maybe the fire department to extricate her. Her prayers had been answered.

Other times, the concept of God, a higher power or order in the universe, takes a beating from one of its own anointed representatives—which can also be hilarious.

I think it was Albert Einstein who said that the idea of God was just too specific for the human mind. Whatever that means, I'm sure I don't know; maybe it's an idea that can only exist in some kind of isolation, where stained glass windows color the only light that gets in. You probably don't want to ask cops about God.

Dispatched to a health food store downtown on a Sunday night, I was about to talk with one of the deity's local representatives.

It was almost midnight, and the owner was claiming that he'd just been robbed. I arrived to find an older white male, about sixty-five, wearing what appeared to be clothing that you'd wear to church: slacks, a white shirt, tie, and dress shoes.

He came to me and reached out to shake my hand. I didn't extend mine; by now, such pleasantries had become suspicious, this one being a common ploy to get the officer to extend his gun hand—and once in a handshake, he's unable to access his sidearm.

He said to me, "Thank you for coming brother."

I looked at him and said, "You assume a lot. Why did you call me here?"

He was annoying me very quickly with his alleged offer of friendship, and now he was calling me his brother? Obviously, this approach had worked for him before.

I asked him for identification, and he took a "temple recommend," as they're called, indicating certified worthiness for entry into his religion's temple, from his shirt pocket and handed it to me. This was only getting more aggravating.

"Do you have any legitimate ID? This is meaningless."

Maybe I shouldn't have said it quite that way, but it later became clear that I was right.

He proceeded to try to tell me that this piece of identification spoke more to his character than any driver's license.

I asked him to please save the shit for someone else. I was well aware of what the document was for, and if he didn't start talking fast, I was leaving.

Frustrated, he paused and just looked at me, glaring. Then he started to tell me what had happened.

He'd come down to the store to do his weekly run to a cheese factory a couple counties over, as he did every Sunday after church services to stock his health food store.

He said that this night he'd come back to the store to unload the cheese, and when he finished he came out to his car and was robbed by a strange female. He said that she took his wallet and wouldn't give it back and that she was in a car right now, parked in front of the store.

This was making no sense.

He says he was robbed after a midnight cheese run by a woman that stayed at the scene? I went to the car and spoke to the woman—and instantly, it all became clear.

She was a prostitute; we'd run into each other many times on the street. Sometimes she gave me information. She'd never lied to me, so I asked her what had happened.

She said that the old man was one of her regular clients and that he liked to have her meet him on Sundays late in the evening after he came back from his cheese runs for his store. This was how he kept their arrangement hidden from his wife; they'd meet at the store, and he'd pay her for whatever sexual act he wanted her to perform that week.

She said that after she was done with him that night, he wouldn't pay her, so she took his wallet. He threatened to call the police, and she told him to go right ahead; she'd wait right there.

I asked her what she wanted done, and she said that all she wanted was the money that he owed her, the money that he'd promised. She hadn't taken anything from his wallet.

I asked her for the wallet, and she gave it to me. I then told her that I'd do what I could but that I couldn't promise anything.

I went back to the old man with his wallet and let him see it.

He reached for it, but I refused to return it until we cleared a few things up.

I asked him why he kept the temple recommend in his shirt pocket and not in his wallet. He said he liked to keep it "closer to his heart."

"Uh huh...is that right?" I replied.

I asked him how the girl had enforced the robbery. "Did she have a weapon? Did she make threats?"

He said that she asked to use his phone inside the business, and as a servant of the Lord he felt it was his duty to help those less fortunate than he, so he let her use it. While he was opening the door to his store, she'd forced him against the door and took the wallet from his pants pocket.

I stared at him for a long while, not saying a word.

Finally, he said, "Are you going to take the word of a prostitute over me?"

I smiled. "How did you know she was a prostitute?"

I'd never mentioned it.

"Look," I said. "I'm gonna make this really clear for you. She's a prostitute. I know her, and so do you. She says that she's been seeing you for some time after your little midnight cheese runs. She also says that you refused to pay her for what she did tonight, and that was why she took your wallet. She didn't take one dime from it and freely gave it back to me."

He interrupted me to say that he was "a high ranking official in his church" and that she was a common whore. Who was I going to believe?

"The common whore," I calmly replied. "You know there's a Supreme Court case that says just because someone's a thief or a whore, whatever, it can't be assumed that they're also a liar...you're probably not interested. Anyway, she's never lied to me, and you haven't told me one word of truth here tonight."

He tried to grab his wallet from me again, stating that he'd had enough and was going home.

"Not yet, you're not. You have some choices to make. First, keeping ID in a shirt pocket is common practice for people who see hookers. See, while she's giving you a blowjob and your pants are down, she has access to your wallet—and most men who frequent hookers know this. After losing their wallet a time or two, they put the important ID in their shirt pocket, where it wouldn't be stolen. Funny how you did just that...keeping it closer to your heart."

He was silent.

"She only wants to be paid," I continued. "If she doesn't get paid, I'm gonna arrest you both. She's been arrested many times, so it will mean nothing to her; you, however, will be front page news."

After growing even quieter, he said, "What do I have to do to keep that from happening, sir?"

"Pay her, which is all she wants—and an apology would be nice. Then I'll clear this call as 'unfounded.' No report will be written, and there won't be any record of all this. The choice is yours."

"I'll pay and apologize," he said. Which he did.

The expression on her face was priceless. Smiling, she went on her way and he went back to his life, temple recommend close to his heart, façade intact.

28 Officer-Assisted Suicide

IT'S A WORTHY GOAL, AN inspirational one, not to get shot, right up there with not having to shoot anyone. One night, I had the chance to work on those career goals.

Working the central city, it was a little slow, and dispatch asked me to take a call on the west side.

The area car, Officer Divot, was busy at the station—most likely getting bodily fluids all over the shoes of management.

It was a car burglary.

Dale Dirk had his car broken into and reported it, and he called back to ask when a cop would be en route; he wanted to get the paperwork done so he could go to bed.

So I headed west, and on the way I asked the dispatcher to call back and find out the apartment number. The address was a little motel just over a bridge, and I knew it fairly well. I didn't usually ask this particular question. If it wasn't a hot call, I liked to walk around first and scout the area to see what was going on, then go to the call; for some reason, though, this time I asked about the apartment.

I was annoyed at the officer who was assigned to the area for not being there, and I also had newly promoted Sgt. Peabody to deal with. He was an ass beyond belief, and we didn't connect—and never would. I was a little irritated and hurried.

As a field-training officer, Peabody had just been an ass; as a sergeant, though, he was an unbearable dickhead. He was controlling and nitpicky and would make huge mistakes that he'd then put on others for not keeping him informed enough to make better decisions.

Peabody had made a career out of blaming his errors on the lack of good info from others; he was quite skilled at it, actually.

I was just turning into the driveway when Barb, the dispatcher, asked where I was. I told her I was just arriving.

She said one word, "Stop," as calm as could be—but in a way that made me jam the brake pedal to the floor.

Barb was probably one of the better dispatchers we had; incredibly competent, knew her shit, and never got ruffled or stressed on the radio. She'd warned me with the mere inflection in her voice.

Barb told me that when she called Dale Dirk, our car burg victim, his father answered the phone. There was no car burglary.

The father stated that his son had been drinking after breaking up with his girlfriend and at that moment was outside with a gun, hiding behind a car and waiting for the cop he called to show up.

He intended to ambush the cop, said his father, trying to provoke a shooting to get himself killed in a suicide-by-cop. This happens often enough, unfortunately.

I looked down the driveway to Dirk's apartment and saw no one; he was still hiding. I put the car in reverse and backed the hell out of there as fast as I could go. I was smoking the tires, hoping not to get shot as I backed up almost an entire city block.

Dirk was waiting with a .357 Magnum handgun, and when he saw me back out he went inside and got on the phone with dispatch, wanting to know where the hell I was going.

While he was on the phone, his Dad fled the apartment.

Dispatch told Dirk what his dad had said, that there was no car burglary, and that he'd told them he just wanted to shoot a cop.

He said, "So?" He wanted to die, and he said he would find a way, then hung up.

Meanwhile, Peabody "super-hero sergeant" was on his way to the scene...praise the Lord, save us all.

He ordered a perimeter set up—which was good—and while he was doing that I was on my cell phone with Dirk, talking to him to try to establish a rapport of some kind.

This pissed Peabody off to no end. He wanted to be in control of the scene and wanted to do the talking himself, so he demanded that I hang up and allow him to talk to Dirk.

I ignored him; I was reaching Dirk, and I wasn't about to turn him over to Peabody.

Peabody then started calling me on the radio, ordering me to hang up so that he could talk to Dirk—and being quite a dick about it.

I had to shut the radio off so I could continue with Dirk, and eventually I did negotiate him out. He came out with his hands up and surrendered.

Instead of being happy about the successful conclusion to the call, though, Peabody went off. He was screaming at me as I was putting Dirk in my car, red face twisted and spitting all over the place.

He felt that I'd undermined his authority—never mind the fact that I'd narrowly missed an ambush, then negotiated the suspect out of the house without a shot being fired and no SWAT call out; I hadn't jumped when "Peabody The Amazing" had said jump.

In the car on the way to jail, I talked with Dirk for some time about his little girl and family. I also showed him pictures of my kids. I wanted him to realize that I had a life as well and that he could have ended that life in addition to his own with stupid shit like this.

He cried in the car and apologized.

Peabody tried to write me up for insubordination; just part of being the department's up-and-coming jackass at the time.

Someone higher up, though, squashed the paperwork.

I never found out who it was, but whoever did it apparently had my back and didn't want me to know about it.

Smarter Than A Sergeant 29

YOU MIGHT BE AMAZED (I know we were) at how often some of the shit bags we chased fell for something known as "Knock and Talk."

It's just like it sounds: officers simply knock on the door of a known criminal's address and try to talk their way in without a warrant.

It never ceased to amaze me how often guys with warrants—who consider themselves career streetwise thugs who never held jobs and were proud of it—would invite police officers inside to talk.

It was a psych game, and it was most effective on drug houses where the suspects have lost any common sense with their prolonged drug abuse.

It was worth a try on just about any place we thought some kind of illegal activity was going on. There was no bluff about having a warrant, just a simple ."..would like to ask you a few questions...need your help on something...where'd you get those shoes?"

The cheese dick suspect who opened the door would always worry that not letting the officer in would draw suspicion—even though things were well past suspicious, just not enough to get a judge to sign a warrant.

Of course, it doesn't work on the real bad asses who know the game—and even the law—and just slam the door.

Once inside, the officer is looking for anything that can lend itself to a warrant under the "plain view" doctrine.

One day, one of our guys pulled the knock and talk on a hotel room downtown where we'd heard drugs were being sold. He got in the door and saw the dope, just lying there on a table, distribution quantity.

That was enough for a warrant.

The officer had legally gained entry and now had to prevent the destruction of evidence, so he called it in and asked for back-up as well.

The dumb ass who opened the door was arrested immediately, but his partner—much wiser and more determined to escape—went out a bathroom window measuring 1 foot by 1 foot.

But he left some ID in the room, and we found he had outstanding warrants, even an NCIC hit, which are felonies only. He had warrants for drug possession and aggravated assault, so it was on.

It was a late Saturday afternoon and things were a little slow, so a lot of units got involved. We were searching everywhere and couldn't find this guy. He was all over the radio, K-9 was out running the dogs, and uniforms were on foot going from house to house, checking sheds and garages and any conceivable hiding place.

No one found anything; it was like this guy just disappeared.

I was on the west end, listening over the radio, and I thought, *What would I do to disappear in the middle of a city? Find the nearest phone and call a cab?*

I suggested this to the sergeant handling the search—Peabody again, an arrogant prick who rode everybody under him hard while ass-kissing everyone above him; you couldn't get his nose out of the chief's ass with a crowbar.

Sergeant Peabody said point blank that the idea was ridiculous.

"Young pup," he told me, "you have a lot to learn about drug dealers and crime in general. Sit back and watch what experience can teach you."

Thrilled at such an opportunity, I walked away, got on my cell phone, and called dispatch on the side. I asked them to check the cab companies (there were only a few) and told them to keep it quiet; I told them what Peabody said and that I didn't want him in my ass for checking this out in spite of his ridicule.

They were more than happy to assist with my hunch, Peabody having made no friends at dispatch either.

They called cabbies and simply asked if a man had been picked up in the vicinity of the hotel in the past twenty minutes—and guess what? They'd picked up a sweaty guy who "just wanted to get out of the area as soon as possible."

Dispatch asked the cabbie where he was and if he could stay on the line with the dispatcher until we could get close. He said he would.

Dispatch was loving this, and when I got in the vicinity of the cab they made sure it went out on the air what we'd done and that I was a block from the suspect—just to rub it in Peabody's face.

I asked for back, and three patrol cars showed up within moments. We picked up the lucky suspect, the one who almost got away, and paid the cabbie for driving slow and working with us.

He'd been alarmed to learn that he had danger in the back seat, and he was glad to join in the capture of the guy.

I was also pretty jacked up.

For a "young pup who had a lot to learn about drug dealers," I was quite happy to be the stupid guy who got it right.

30 Left Hook/Right Guard

GIVEN THE RIGHT CIRCUMSTANCE AND opportunity, anything can be used as a weapon.

I was called to a family fight, but when I arrived it was already over. At the scene, I found a small, compact woman who claimed her husband had been out with another woman. She also claimed that he'd attacked her when she confronted him about the affair, saying that he threw her around the room and left.

Surprisingly, she seemed unhurt with only a few minor abrasions showing.

As I started to take the information from her about what had happened and what his name was, he walked in.

More than a foot taller than his wife, he was a mess, covered in blood.

When I asked him what had happened, he described coming home from a friend's house to have his wife accuse him of being with another woman. He told her that was ridiculous—then she attacked him, a barely five-foot package of woman, enraged.

He said she hit him in the head over and over again with a metal spray can. She chased him all through the house until he was able to lock himself in the bathroom. She then grabbed a knife and drove it through the wooden bathroom door several times, trying to get at him.

Growing impatient with that approach, she brought out a bag of charcoal and a can of lighter fluid, then poured it all out around the base of the door and tried to light it while screaming, "I'm gonna fucking KILL your white ass! Nobody fucks around on me!"

When he smelled the lighter fluid and saw smoke, he said he panicked. He knew if she got her planned barbecue going, he'd be trapped with no escape, so he opened the door and blew past her. Running as fast as he could, he knocked her down as he fled out the front door.

Deep semi-circular cuts were easily visible all over his head, some right down to the bone and still bleeding.

I called for medical and checked the bathroom; charcoal was all around the base of the doorway, wet with liquid that smelled like charcoal lighter.

I went back to the woman, now sitting quietly on the couch. I tried to get her explanation for the charcoal and the cuts on her husband's head, but she refused to talk.

I reached to grab her arm to get her attention as she sat catatonic on the couch—and the touch caused her to turn into a screaming crazy woman, jumping and flailing, scratching and biting.

I was able to get her to the floor and handcuff her.

I checked the couch and found the metal aerosol can: a "Right Guard" brand spray can. It had strands of hair and blood on the bottom edges.

I arrested her for aggravated assault and attempted arson, then booked her into jail.

A week later, they were back together again, walking down the street.

When I saw them, I called the prosecutors, who told me that the charges had been dropped; he'd refused to testify against her... imagine that.

31 Triangulated

ONE NIGHT, I WAS GETTING in some overtime "cleaning up the board," as the sergeants called it, meaning I'd take all the non-priority calls running all over the city to get them off the dispatch logs as soon as possible.

It made our stats look good, and it got me out of my assigned area for a while. For us, it's a chance for some freelancing, cruising around putting out minor fires, nothing too serious; but this night, that didn't last long.

A call came in from a gas station near the eastern foothills that promised some guy looking for a confrontation, preferably with the cops.

The caller dialed 911 to say that he was "Wyatt Earp" and that we'd better get up there fast. He said he had a knife, and then he hung up and waited.

I was on the west side, listening; it sounded like trouble, so I started towards the location.

I was about halfway there when officers on the scene radioed, yelling for help; meanwhile, Mr. Earp's girlfriend had called dispatch to say that he was suicidal and wanted to provoke the police into shooting him.

I was next to arrive and found a patrolman and a sergeant backing away from Earp, who was walking around with a huge fucking blade, a big Bowie knife. The scent of pepper spray was in the air; it was already tried on Earp with no effect.

He kept advancing on the two officers, ignoring any attempts to talk him down. I yelled to get his attention, and he started towards me.

I had a car between us, and we actually ran around it a few times—him chasing me and me pepper-spraying him. The spray continued to have no effect; he just wiped it off and kept coming, closing in on me. (This was a few years before Tasers.)

I backed away from the car and pulled out my Glock, trying to talk him down, but he wouldn't respond; he just kept coming at me with that huge knife, head down, eyes locked on mine.

It was easy to see him gutting me with no regrets, so I settled into a firing stance.

Just then, the other two officers fell in behind him. We were all in each other's field of fire; triangulated, but a flat triangle.

So, I holstered up and got ready to fight, go toe to toe—"going toes" as we called it. He kept closing in, still quiet and determined.

It was terrifying.

The sound of your blood rushing in your ears isn't fiction; there's a background buzz, a hazy noise as your metabolism launches with adrenaline, preparing you for battle.

This guy wasn't swinging the knife where I could grab for his arm and hold on; instead, he held it close to his body, which would make it very hard to fight him and come out of this without my guts dumped all over the pavement.

Realizing I was about to get seriously fucked up, my pulse elevated; I was getting angry, getting ready to rip this guy apart.

Rage and fear are powerful emotions, and even more volatile when mixed. I wasn't going to die. Not in my mind. I envisioned crushing his throat and ripping out his eyes; losing this battle was *not* an option.

Then out of nowhere, Bobby Grimes drove his patrol car between me and Earp, hitting Earp with a glancing blow from the car—which probably saved my life. I couldn't believe it.

Earp was furious, and he viciously attacked the car, striking the driver's window over and over.

Sparks flew from the metal frame around the door glass, and then the door, as he tried to smash his way through to get at Grimes. With Bobby behind the determined attacker, I still didn't have a shot.

Earp eventually tired of trying to kill Grimes in the car, and turned back towards the other two officers. Grimes was then able to get out of the car, and we both approached Earp.

Fortunately, Grimes had a shot and took it.

He double-tapped Earp, hitting him twice in the torso, which immediately dropped him to the ground.

I holstered and started first aid, calling dispatch to send medical. Earp, his real name Darin Eest, was gasping doing what was called agonal breathing, the last gasps.

He died at the scene, and the press crucified Grimes because some eyewitness who was an ex-con claimed that Eest had no knife; he said that the one we reported had been planted.

The guys in the department talked a lot of shit about Grimes as well; after an incident like this, you find out really quickly that you have very few friends in police work.

The Internal Affairs investigation was grueling.

The IA investigator asked me why I hadn't shot Eest.

I explained that I couldn't because of the background; in the rush of events, we were in each other's way and our triangulation stressed.

Every time I had a shot, an officer would turn up behind Eest.

"So you're trying to tell me that every time you had a shot, another officer stepped behind the suspect and put himself in jeopardy, seeing that your gun was out and pointed in his direction?" he asked.

"I can't tell you what he saw," I answered. "You know, Eest never did stop to ask us where we wanted him to stand. It was a fluid situation."

The department seemed to be looking for a way to rule it as a bad shoot, but eventually Grimes was cleared and he came back to work.

I always had a hard time around Bobby after that. He saved my life, and I could never repay him.

The department and the media treated him poorly. He suffered. He cried over killing that kid; Bobby was as solid as they come, brave as hell, tough, smart—but he cried over this guy.

I even heard that his wife was spat on in a grocery store by a group of people who called Bobby a killer. I was enraged by what he was going through.

It turned out that the department hadn't even read my report on the shooting; I had to go in and explain it to one of the lieutenants, telling him about how he'd saved my life.

I put him in for a Medal of Valor, but it was repeatedly denied.

I raised hell with anyone who'd listen, but the bottom line was that the brass didn't like Bobby. I was almost fired for insubordination, having pushed against the sergeant on the scene at the time of the incident and then the duty lieutenant who worked that night.

I wouldn't let it go; they had to make this right.

They finally did, but I had to go over some heads to an assistant chief to get heard, further cementing my lack of popularity.

I'd never had anyone step up during a life-threatening situation and help me like Bobby had.

32 Something For The Trophy Case

STARTING OUT ON A SLOW night that was about to heat up, I was babysitting a bank parking lot. As you might imagine, when bankers complain, the department responds.

The financial hub was just off Main Street, which the kids like to traverse, "Cruising The Boulevard," as it's called.

Cruising involves various collection points where the kids can pull off and gather, and well-kept parking lots such as a bank's are very popular. The bank was having a lot of problems with the kids partying there, leaving a lot of trash and usually causing some property damage.

So often, this is a simple matter to solve; just park a patrol car there. This also worked in moving the hookers around.

When an establishment complains that too many of the working girls are hanging out, just have a uniformed officer park in the area; instantly, they relocate. These are just nuisance calls.

Same with boulevard cruisers who congregate in parking lots to talk and compare cars. If they're trashing the place, just having a patrol car take up residency solves what's largely a litter problem and moves them along. We're not garbage men.

I was camped out in the bank parking lot this night when I saw a trooper in a chase with Jack Converse; they went flying past me, westbound across Main.

I knew Jack, a troubled kid. I grew up with his dad, an abusive alcoholic providing nothing but a volatile home life for Jack. I saw Jack as a nice kid who had little chance at any kind of normal life; this night, he gave up.

The troopers didn't have access to our radio frequencies back then, and we weren't able to hear theirs; so, I called in the chase with dispatch and tried to parallel them, attempting to catch up.

They zigzagged back and forth in the area, and I couldn't find them.

Then they turned east, crossing Main again, going up four blocks and back into the inner city again before I finally caught up with them.

As I rounded the corner, I saw that both Jack and the trooper were out of their vehicles, facing each other with guns drawn.

The trooper backed off some, waiting for backup and moving closer to his cruiser, leaving Jack standing out in the middle of the street, defiant and emboldened.

I got out and challenged him from about sixty feet away.

He started to move toward the sidewalk, and I moved to cut him off.

Another patrol car arrived, and with the trooper we had him cornered. Jack wouldn't back down, though, instead ignoring commands and waving his gun around.

I had no idea why he ran on the trooper, but this was now something else. Why wouldn't he just put his gun down and surrender? This was a little more obvious; it appeared that he wanted to die...he knew what he was setting himself up for.

He pointed the gun first at the trooper, then at the other patrolman. Finally, he settled on me.

We'd spoken just a few weeks earlier, friendly talking about the trouble he was drifting into. I don't know if it was his interest in gangs or drugs that was driving him, or more likely that he just didn't like going home before his virulent, alcoholic father passed out for the night.

He was barely eighteen, but I think somehow in this fucked up world he found himself in, he wanted to die.

He was no longer just pointing the gun, but decidedly aiming at me.

I fired four times, the other officers firing almost simultaneously.

The shooting was strangely quiet for me; I only heard my gun go off. The patrol cars all had their sirens on, but I never heard any of that.

I never heard the other guys' guns go off, either.

All I had in focus was Jack aiming at me, and that was what I concentrated on.

He dropped to the ground, and I started First Aid.

The shoot bothered me only in that I knew where Jack was coming from and what his life was like. It still left me numb.

Jack was looking for his way out—through me. I had no desire to kill or hurt him; I just wanted to live myself.

What was also burned into my consciousness from that night was my sergeant, Leeds again. He turned on me, fearing I had a leg up on him as he'd never had what he saw as the "macho romance" of a shootout.

From that point on, he actively went after me every chance he got.

He was one sick fuck, angry that his career ended years later without ever shooting anyone, leaving his trophy case apparently empty.

Jack lived.

On the way home that night, I called the hospital and checked on him. Two of his fingers had been shot off, one round went into his chest, and another blew his dick off. At the hospital, they laughed that they'd roughly cleaned up the injured gangster without an anesthetic.

I hung up, no longer sure what planet I was on.

Once healed, Jack was sent to prison.

A little later, one of the patrolmen contacted me to say that they were removing a bullet from an inmate I shot and wanted to know if I needed it as a memento. It wasn't mine, and why would I want it if it were?

The Chief And Parking 33

ONE DAY I CAME TO work and, sitting in the afternoon briefing, heard this: we were told that under no circumstances would we be parking against traffic in the city from that day forward.

We all looked at each other, puzzled at such a ridiculous statement.

We asked why this was being brought up. There had to be a reason to contradict the state law that said we could violate any traffic law necessary to effect an arrest or come to the aid of a citizen or another officer—so what was up?

It turned out that the Chief had been chewed out by the city council for someone parking against traffic. He felt threatened by it and felt that his job was in jeopardy.

We were told that his exact words were that he "would not go down for this alone." If anyone was caught parking against traffic, they'd be given days off without pay and lose the privilege of the take-home patrol car.

We were getting used to this from the Chief; everything that happened was about him, how it related to him, and how he was perceived in the press and by the city council.

He didn't look out for the best interests of the department; he just looked out for his own best interests.

He'd been self-centered as a sergeant and a lieutenant, and now as a Chief he was unbearable.

So we left the briefing, and right out of the office I got a call; it was a woman and a man in a dispute over property in one of the poorer parts of the city.

I headed out east bound, then arrived and saw a woman pushing a shopping cart full of her possessions. She was almost to the intersection of a main street, only one or two houses west of it, and she was in a heated argument with a large white male. He was extremely animated and shoved her a couple times, slamming her into her cart.

I caught a break in traffic, then cut across, parked against the traffic, got out, and interrupted the fight, stopping it before it really got out of hand.

There was a crowd gathering to watch the possible fight, and I dispersed them.

I was busy dealing with the two people.

The woman had called and wanted her things from the guy, who happened to be her landlord; it was a civil case, which is always a pain in the ass.

She was basically going to be homeless because the landlord wanted his rent money and had legally evicted her.

I was there as a mediator, trying to get the two upset adults back into "adult mode" thinking, back into reality, and I was just about finished when Sgt. Gus walked up.

Looking upset, he said to me, "Are you almost done?"

I said that I was. He said good and told me to meet him in the station when I was done. I had no idea why, but I could tell it wasn't good.

Turned out, the Chief drove past the call while I was parked against traffic—and he was furious.

He sent out orders to have both me and my Sgt. relieved of duty for not obeying his "order" about parking against traffic.

I spent the rest of the shift writing and explaining to Sgt. Gus and the Duty Lieutenant why I did what I did.

I didn't do it to challenge the Chief; I did it to protect the woman from getting her ass kicked.

I made sure that I quoted state law and explained what I did with the public's well-being in mind.

When I left that day, I was relieved of duty, as was Sgt. Gus. The Sergeant and the Duty Lieutenant both said, though, that they thought that I'd acted correctly and that the Chief was really out of line.

By the next afternoon, I was back on duty and all punishment had been dropped for both Sgt. Gus and me.

Apparently, the senior staff had confronted the Chief and told him that they wouldn't support his action.

They also told him that he'd have a revolt from within the department if he continued to punish us for taking the correct action in protecting the public and doing our duty.

I heard that the final deciding factor for the Chief was that, if it got out to the press, it would be really hard to explain that one of the officers had put himself in danger to protect a citizen, driving against and parking against traffic due to the emergent nature of the situation and breaking up a fight in progress between a homeless woman and her landlord—only to have the Chief drive by afterward and second guess that decision.

Once again, the Chief chose what was best for himself and dropped it. No apology, no explanation; it was just dropped.

The police department really didn't like our Chief; he constantly butted heads with everyone. He even refused to pay us during the Y2K scare.

We were required to be on call and had to make plans for our families to be taken care of should the power grids fail and civilization as we knew it fall; seriously, they really overreacted to this, and we were on 12-hour shifts and on call.

We were required to be reimbursed for being on call, as well as for the overtime for the 12-hour shifts, but the Chief refused to pay us out of his budget. He wanted it come out of the city's budget.

He called a mandatory meeting—which we had to be paid for as well—and told us all point blank that he wouldn't pay us for the extra time.

He said, "If you don't like it, then sue me. I don't care; I'm not paying."

This was his idea of employee relations.

We did start a class action lawsuit, after which the city wisely decided to pay us.

To make matters worse between the Chief and me, I ran into another Chief I knew from another department.

The chiefs have a yearly meeting where they all get together, and in this meeting my Chief was bragging about what good shots his officers were. He asked me if it was true that one of the guys intentionally shot a guy's dick off...I was speechless.

I'd made that shot on purpose, yes.

Being sixty feet away, I thought I was missing Jack Converse during the shooting; so, I lowered my weapon's aim to the groin area, thinking that I was shooting high because that's common at night. Jack had suffered the consequences.

To hear that the Chief was bragging about this in a Chiefs' meeting somewhere, I was shocked, angry, and now disliked him even more.

He never even so much as acknowledged me in the hallways at work, but he'd take credit for my work at Chiefs' meetings as if he were in some way responsible for anything I did.

Shoplifting A Rap Bag 34

ONE NIGHT, I WAS CALLED to a large grocery store that was in the central part of the city.

Store security had observed a man shoplifting and had detained him; they said they had a shoplifter in custody who had stolen a rap magazine.

I arrived and contacted security, and they took me back to their office in the rear of the store. It was about eight feet wide by ten deep, just big enough for a desk and a couple chairs.

They introduced me to a stocky muscular guy who identified himself as James Gray.

I asked Gray for identification, and he said that he had none; he claimed that he had no identification at all.

That was a problem for me because I couldn't release him on a misdemeanor citation if I couldn't positively identify him with legitimate identification.

I wrote down all the necessary information from the security guards and Mr. Gray, then asked him to stand up and turn around.

He stood up but didn't turn around; instead, he said, "What the fuck is this?"

I explained to him that without identification I couldn't give him a citation and that I had to book him into jail for the $2 magazine.

He said, "Fuck that. I ain't going to jail, motherfucker."

I told him again to turn around and tried to turn him, but he refused—and the fight was on.

He was really quite strong; I'd later find out that he'd just gotten out of prison and knew that this theft would violate his parole—and he was willing to do almost anything to avoid going back to prison.

We fought pretty hard for some time.

I slammed his head into the walls, destroying the drywall and really making a mess out of the security office.

Finally, I managed to call for back up, and I heard a couple officers acknowledge and claim that they were en route.

We were then back at it, fighting and wrestling, until finally I was able to get him cuffed.

We were both covered with the white powder from the dry wall, and we looked like hell.

The security officers had just backed out of the room when the fight broke out.

They were scared of Gray; he was pretty buff and very intimidating.

I cleaned up, and when I'd rested up enough I asked Gray what the hell the problem was, why the hell was he fighting so hard over a stupid shoplifting charge?

He then told me that he was on paper and would violate his parole and he would most likely be sent back to prison.

Then I understood at least why he acted the way he did.

I talked to him for a few minutes and found out that his family was outside in the parking lot, waiting for him.

Even though he was cuffed and had lost the fight, he was still combative, angry, and trying to get away.

He kicked at me a couple times and tried to head butt me—and finally I had enough.

I grabbed him by the head and slammed it into the wall a couple times—hard.

This broke the drywall, punching a hole in it through the other side; his head was now sticking out in the storage area of the store.

I pulled him back out of the hole and told him that he had a choice to make: he could either leave the store walking, or I'd drag him out like a fucking dog in front of his kids and everyone else.

This struck him hard; he didn't want his kids to see him that way, so he quit fighting and asked that I clean him up and let him say goodbye to his sons.

I agreed but made it clear that if he changed his mind, I'd embarrass him as much as I could in front of his family.

I cleaned him up as much as I could, and he did cooperate, so I let him say goodbye to his sons.

When we got into the car, he thanked me and apologized for fighting me.

He said that he thought that he could take me since it was just him and me fighting.

No other cops had shown up and helped out.

They'd shown up in the parking lot and signed out on the radio claiming that they were there, but they never got out of their cars; instead, they waited in the parking lot in their cars while I was fighting inside the building.

Two units were in the parking lot...so much for the thin blue line.

Years later, I was training a new guy on the midnight shift.

He told me that he was a security guard at that same grocery store in central city and that he'd "seen it all" working there.

He then started to tell me this incredible story about a shoplifter who had refused to submit to arrest.

He said that the cop was smaller than the shoplifter and that he destroyed their store's security office arresting him.

He said they talked about it for months, about how it had happened and how the guy's head went into the drywall.

He told me the whole story from his point of view, recalling how terrified he was of the shoplifter, then later how afraid he was of the cop.

I never told him it was me.

It never ceased to amaze me how others saw the things that were just a normal part of the job for me.

35 Burning House Entry

ONE NIGHT, I WAS ADVISED by dispatch that there was a report of a house fire in my area.

Dispatch would often give us a heads-up on medicals and house fires so that we could help out with traffic control and securing the scene before medical arrived.

Usually, we were too busy to help out unless it was really bad; however, this night had been slow.

When I arrived, there were a couple cars already there.

The cops were out of their cars, watching the fire.

The building was a house that had been remodeled, and it was now a duplex, one apartment up and one apartment down.

The downstairs apartment was fully engulfed by the fire.

Everyone knew the upstairs was occupied by a group of ten to twelve Mexicans, most likely illegal immigrants working to support their families in Mexico; we'd been to that apartment several times on loud parties.

I got out and asked the group of cops that was there if anyone had exited the upstairs apartment.

They said that no one had come out since they'd been there.

I was a bit anxious; I wasn't going to sit back and watch while a bunch of people burned to death.

I asked, "Well are we going in?"

They said that they "weren't going in to rescue a bunch of Mexicans."

I started towards the house, and they yelled "we aren't gonna save your ass for a bunch of Mexicans either...you're going alone."

I kept going.

Another officer ran up to me and said, "What the hell are you doing? You're gonna die in there!"

I turned to him and said, "I'm not gonna sit out here and watch while they burn to death when I could have done something. I won't live like that; I won't have this shit on my conscience."

He grabbed my arm and said, "They're just Mexicans."

I broke free from him and started up the stairs to the apartment above the fire, and he started to cry.

He was scared to death but said, "Wait! Then...OK...I'll go with you."

We went in and got the people out long before the fire department arrived.

I was really scared that the fire had burned out enough of the floor in the top apartment that once we entered we'd fall through to the fire below.

He cursed me the whole time we were in the burning house; it was hot and smoky and really hard to see, and we were coughing hard while we searched on our hands and knees to make sure they were all out.

When we finally got back outside, I left.

The other officers shook their heads, watching us exit the house; they weren't impressed at all at what they felt was my stupidity.

Later, the guy who went in with me would approach me.

He was still mad, and he said to me, "You are fucking crazy. I heard this about you—that you do this stupid shit! You could have gotten us killed!"

It was days like this that made me feel like I lived in a different universe.

36 Joe's Perfect Camaro

THERE WAS A GUY NAMED Joe in the inner city who had a really sweet '68 Camaro.

He'd put a lot of work into it, and it was amazingly nice.

I used to stop and talk to him while he worked on it.

He was married and had a couple kids. His wife wasn't as excited about the car as I was, and she didn't like me showing up and praising the work he did.

One day, I caught a call for a car that had driven through the front porch of a house, then crashed into a tree.

I arrived, and there was Joe's Camaro wrapped around a tree—completely totaled. It was a sad thing to see.

I started to interview people and found out that the driver had been Joe. I couldn't believe it.

Witnesses said that he'd come out of his apartment, got into the car, and started it, revving the motor. Then he drove it through the front porch of a neighbor's house.

He continued down the driveway and across the street into the tree, then got out and ran back to his apartment.

I went to the apartment and knocked on the door.

His wife answered.

She was beaten up and just pointed into the apartment and said, "He's in there. Get him the fuck out of here."

I went into the apartment and found Joe.

He was covered in sweat and drooling. I'd never seen him that way.

I put him in handcuffs and walked him out of the door.

His wife denied medical treatment for her injuries; she just wanted him out of their apartment.

I took him to jail, and on the way he started to hallucinate.

While in jail, he started seeing bugs crawling on the walls and screamed that they were on him; I couldn't complete the paperwork with him wigging out next to me.

The other officers in the booking area were really uncomfortable with him acting this way as well, so I decided to put him into a holding cell and asked the booking officers to open one up.

I put him in the cell as he ranted and raved about the bugs on him, then closed the door, sat back down, and went back to work on the paperwork.

About ten minutes passed, and I was almost done—when it became really quiet in the holding cell.

I looked up, and the other officers also stopped and we all looked at each other, waiting, listening.

After a few seconds, I got up and went to check on Joe.

I looked through the holding cell door window, and there was Joe. He was on his knees, his head in the steel toilet, hands still cuffed behind his back. I thought that he was trying to kill himself.

What I did not know was that the holding cell plumbing had been inoperable for several days. Someone on one of the floors above the cell had flushed rolls of toilet paper down the toilet.

It is a way that inmates try to fight back against the system. (Minor passive aggressive actions that cause disruption for the correctional officers.)

Anyway, the toilet had not been working for several days. It had filled up with shit, piss, and vomit during those three days and Joe had his head buried in it.

I yelled at the booking officers and told them to open the holding cell.

I went inside and yelled at Joe.

As I entered the cell yelling at him, he pulled his head out of the disgusting muck in the toilet.

Shit and chunks of vomit running down his face and in his teeth, mouth and nose.

I said "What the hell are you doing?"

He turned and looked at me and said, "I was thirsty!"

This was by far one of the most amazingly disgusting things I had ever witnessed.

The correctional officers came in and hosed him off and I finished booking him into jail.

I was amazed at his behavior. It is shocking what tweekers are capable of doing after a couple of weeks without sleep.

Bat Shit Crazy 37

IT WAS NEVER MORE APPARENT that I was not like the rest of the guys I worked with than when we went to training.

Guys who are proud to display on their office walls the certificates of expertise they have earned usually conduct training for Law enforcement.

They have impeccable resumes, and impressive credentials. Basically mirroring academia in the belief that certificates, public accolades, and successful course completion equates to valuable real world experience. It does not.

The expert on the street is the guy who survived the previous night.

Every night is a challenge to adapt to an ever-increasingly hostile and complicated series of obstacles. The fact you continue your employment and survive the battles on the street both mentally and physically is a testament to your expertise.

Not the trophy wall, not the resume proudly displayed on line. Your resume is a series of successful returns to your home and family.

Regardless, the law requires that cops be trained in the "latest" techniques thought up by Law enforcement "experts".

In our state a minimum amount of training was required by Law and it was a budget challenge to figure out how to keep the training hours up and costs down.

The idea should have been to get the most bang for your buck. Instead for a period of time it was to get the cheapest training possible. This made for some interesting classes, taught by the "I love me" cops.

One option our department tried out for a time was a televised network of training classes. We would be required to pile into the department's training room and listen to the latest self proclaimed expert teach us the latest "critical skill".

One day I was sitting in class listening to the latest most amazing important skill I was supposed to master and trying desperately hard to not fall asleep.

The classes were tedious as hell and if you were a critical thinker at all you could see huge faults in the training logic.

I had been taught many years ago by one of the best cops I had ever met to challenge anything and everything you were taught. If it made no sense or if you could not modify it or make it work for you, dump it and move on.

His mentoring me would be a huge influence on my survival in the field.

The idea of 'questioning everything mentality' would rub a lot of people I worked with the wrong way and I would always be on the outside of the "good ole boy network" looking in.

The cop who mentored me was Robert Suggs. He will get his own story much later on in these books.

Today's class was about surviving a hostage situation as a cop.

If you were ever taken hostage as a cop what would your plan of survival be? Basically planning for the worst situation possible.

The scenario was spelled out like this; you were handcuffed and disarmed and being held hostage. How would you escape and overcome your captors?

The televised training went on and on about mentally preparing your self for this unbelievable eventuality.

One of the questions asked in the class was if you were ever in a situation where you were told to surrender your weapon or the bad guy would shoot another officer what would you do? The situation actually did happen occasionally.

One guy I worked with had been held hostage, he and another cop were tied up and told they were about to be shot in the head.

Somehow they escaped and physically survived the situation.

Mentally though he was damaged. He was scared for the rest of his career and would never respond to dangerous calls with the same sense of urgency.

He was terrified of being held hostage again.

I don't know what happened, I was not there, but I saw how it affected him.

The trainer did not make any recommendations about what your course of action should be, he just asked that we consider what our choices would be if it did happen.

The guy who was instructing the televised class said that he recommended that all cops keep several hand cuff keys on them at all times. He thought this was a good idea whether you were on duty or off. He then detailed the six different places he kept a handcuff key on him at all times.

Usually I kept my opinions about the training to myself. I had made comments before and I had been harshly rebuked and told I knew nothing, I was a rookie and I should keep my mouth shut.

I could not keep it in any longer though and finally erupted in a tirade against what I felt was not only stupid training but dangerous training.

My personal opinion is to always be on the offensive in any situation, not planning how to survive a seriously stupid mistake.

Don't make the mistake in the first place and you don't have to be a walking poster boy for a key fetish.

I voiced this opinion and immediately I could see the guy next to me was offended, His name was Tim Mathues.

Tim Mathues was a mystery to me and I admit I never really got my head around how he thought about being a cop.

He had been raised in a rural environment where I had been raised in the city. He was a strict rule follower, I mean to the letter. He followed every policy the department had in place to the letter.

I took great joy in breaking as many rules as I could.

Tim was one of my FTO (Field Training Officers) and he taught me everything I would never want to be.

Sometimes training was like that as well. You learned what you did not want to become.

Anyway one day while I was riding with Tim I made the mistake of calling him Tim.

He stopped the car in the middle of the street abruptly, hands gripping the steering wheel in a white knuckle death grip, while his breathing reached an alarming rate.

I thought he was having an anxiety attack. I was wrong.

He was having a temper tantrum.

He looked at me, red in the face and gritting his teeth, said "NEVER CALL ME TIM!"

He said, Tim was his father's name and he was named after his father.

I said, "Ok Tim what should I call you then?"

Rage, pure rage exploded from Tim and he screamed, "TIMOTHY! I AM TIMOTHY, NOT TIM!"

I was sitting next to him in a full size car.

I could hear him clearly.

I could also see that he had a serious need for some extensive dental work on his molars. His mouth was open that wide as he screamed this in my face.

I realized at that moment Tim was BAT SHIT CRAZY and could probably be the next character in a Stephen King Novel.

I quit tormenting the mentally unstable officer and started to watch him, trying to figure him out.

I was never able to. He was erratic and emotional and never had the same response to any situation.

So I was sitting next to Tim in training and he turned to me and said, "You don't see the value in this training? Do you know why that is?"

I said, "Ya, this is stupid! Do you really think that hiding handcuff keys all over your body is gonna save you? Hell with that! How about making sure that you are never in that situation to begin with?"

He said, "You don't see the value in the training because you don't see the danger in this job. For you this job is a just that, a JOB.

"To those of us who take the job seriously it is more than that, it is a calling, a profession, something to be proud of.

"I listen to the ideas presented in these classes and take them to heart. I want to learn from others and better myself. I plan to be the best cop I can be."

His face was turning red as he talked.

I said, "Look, if you want to hide keys all over your body great! What if you get tied up with zipcuffs, or rope, then what?"

Tim was getting pumped up and the wind was definitely in his sails.

He went on and on about how being prepared for the unexpected was the most important thing a cop could do to survive.

By now our conversation had followers, several of the administration were listening and Tim knew this.

He was sure they agreed with him and I think that he was right.

He started to explain to me that he had hidden keys on his uniform and in his shoes for years now, just in case he was ever taken hostage.

I saw several of the older guys nod their heads in approval.

I asked "How many keys do you carry?" Curious how deep this fear went for him.

He said that he carried seven keys at all times.

I said, "Seven? No shit? Where do you hide all of them?" Pretending to be interested in the way he hid them. Really I was interested in where and why.

I had an idea I would learn more from that information and how he had thought this through than the actual number of keys he kept.

Tim detailed each location and as he did he explained why he kept the key there.

The administrators who were present listened intently to his explanation and I saw several heads nod with approval and smiles were exchanged in agreement with Tim's logic.

Tim reached Key number six and stopped. He just stopped and looked at me.

I said, "Ok that was six, where do you keep the last one?"

Tim was quiet.

I said "Well?"

Tim said, "I get a piece of tape and tape it to my body."

I could tell there was a lot more to this than met the eye.

His body language and demeanor told me that he felt proud of the thought put into the location this taped key.

Tim said that he figured that if he was ever to be taken hostage the only way to defeat his preparations and placement of hidden keys all over his body and in his equipment was to take him hostage in the nude.

He said that he had thought this out and that if he ever was taken hostage and stripped nude he would want to be able to escape.

He also felt that most likely the incident would include another cop also being taken hostage.

He felt that he had to take his preparations seriously, as both of their lives would depend on his planning and forethought.

The administration was extremely impressed by this depth of planning and Tim's commitment to tactical survival.

I was not, but I said nothing.

I said, "Ok, I see what you are getting at. Why would you go to all of this preparation to have it all defeated by simply removing the places you hide the keys? So where do you hide it?"

Tim stood tall in the training room and began to detail the thought process behind this.

He said he pictured himself and another cop naked and hand cuffed in a dark and dirty room. (Really? Seriously?)

They would be handcuffed behind their backs and being naked limited their ability to both hide keys and recover and use them.

He said that he finally figured out that he had to hide a key where it could not be seen but you could access it.

I was thinking to myself, here we go! Bat shit crazy is about to emerge again.

Tim said that he taped the seventh key to his scrotum.

I was speechless, I looked at the administration who were listening, their eyebrows all raised simultaneously in surprise.

I said, "What, you tape it where?"

He said, "You heard me!"

Louder now, and proudly, he said, "I tape the key to my scrotum. That way if I was ever handcuffed behind my back and was with another officer all I would have to do is bend over and the other officer could reach the key if his hands were behind his back."

The room was silent.

I could see the image playing out in the administrator's minds. Furrowed brows emerged as veterans became uncomfortable with the images starting to develop in their minds.

I burst out laughing.

I could not believe the level of paranoia Tim lived with.

This disclosure about his perceived planning for the worst seemed to incorporate more dark hidden sexual fantasy than real fear.

I could not stop laughing. The more I laughed the madder Tim became.

Then I said, "So Tim," knowing this would push him over the edge, "you have a key taped to your nuts right now don't you? I mean we are in training and there is no threat here, but when you came to class today you had a key taped to your nuts right?"

Tim unleashed the I am not Tim, call me Timothy speech I had received before.

Screaming at the top of his lungs, red in the face with veins popping out all over his neck and forehead.

In this context however it just did not sound the same. The administration suddenly had a different perception of Tim.

Looks of surprise and shock replaced their looks of approval.

Tim was bat shit crazy and a great example of the guys I worked with.

People have often asked me why I didn't feel like I fit in with the other cops. I tell them this story and ask, "Would you?"

A SPECIAL PREVIEW OF

RELOAD

ZACH FORTIER

1 Street Creds Preview: Capped In The Ass

YOU KNOW HOW YOU HEAR about bangers always talking shit about "bustin' caps in some fool's ass"? Well, sometimes they mean it!

Doughboy from St. Pauls 13 had just come home on a home visit. He'd been in a Proctor home in San Marcos by court order, and he was allowed to go home on rare occasions to see his mom. He'd been home in the city less than 24 hours when this shooting happened (it's also noteworthy that while he was in San Marcos, they had numerous drive-by shootings and gang activity increased noticeably...hmm...wonder why that was?).

Anyway, Doughboy met up with Roberto Vega, another SP-13 gang member that had been in another "rehab program" back east. They hung out at Vega's house, playing video games for a while, then decided go for a walk to another friend's house. Both Vega and Doughboy had been out of the city for several months, so they went out walking in their old neighborhoods, talking about the girls they'd met during the time they'd been gone and comparing notes on their latest sexual conquests. Suddenly, they ran into several South Side 18th Street gang members, Neto Arredondo and his cousins.

Arredondo was South Side 18th Street and had it tattooed on his chest. He was very proud of his gang membership, but his parents hoped it was a phase that he would soon outgrow. This particular day, his family was having a wedding. His sister was getting married, and he and his cousins had come to the house to get wedding decorations. They were standing in the front yard of Arredondo's house, taking a smoke break from loading their truck. As Doughboy and Vega walked by, the two groups exchanged words. It started out with "Whatchu claim, man?", then went downhill fast from there. They were sworn rivals that hated each other by their gang affiliations.

Doughboy was a huge kid; at 16, he looked like a 35-year-old man. He was 5'8" and easily 250 lbs.—and he feared no one on the streets. He was one of only two Black kids that claimed St. Pauls 13 at the time; the other was already in prison for a shooting. Black kids in St. Pauls 13 were rare since it was a Hispanic gang homegrown and unique to St. Pauls.

Most Black gang members in the city ended up as Crips or Bloods; Dough, however, had grown up hanging out with the homegrown Hispanics and felt an allegiance both to them and the Blacks in the city. He was a very unique guy in a lot of ways.

Anyway, Doughboy jumped the small fence in the front of the house and called the Arredondos out to fight. St. Pauls 13 called the 18th Street gang members "in-betweeners" and sometimes "sewer rats"; 18th Street, on the other hand, called the SP-13 members "Chochas", "Dirtheads", or "Fakers." So, Doughboy challenged the "sewer rats" to a fight. The South Side 18th Street members outnumbered him, but he was huge—and he could fight.

The 18th Street members kept talking shit to him as they backed away, telling him to get the fuck off their property and get the fuck out of there. Meanwhile, Arredondo went around the back of the house and went inside to get his father's 44 mag. He then came out the front door of the house and confronted Dough, telling him to "get the fuck off of his property" or he'd kill him. Doughboy called his bluff and stood his ground, talking shit back to Arredondo and telling him that he was going to kick his ass for trying to scare him with some fake ass gun.

That was a huge mistake—because Arredondo wasn't bluffing. He shot one round at Doughboy's head, narrowly missing it; the round ended up burying itself deep into the telephone pole behind Doughboy and to his left. At that point, Doughboy quickly realized that maybe it was time to leave, so he turned and tried to run, jumping the short fence with Arredondo in pursuit. Doughboy took a couple steps, and Arredondo shot again; this time, he hit Dough right in the ass, the bullet driving deep into the muscle of his right ass cheek. The bullet's impact was so forceful, it knocked Dough right out of his shoes. Still, he continued running as fast as he could, limping now and bleeding. Arredondo shot one more round at Dough as he ran past another telephone pole, again narrowly missing his head; the third round also got buried in the telephone pole.

Meanwhile, Vega was in high-speed "get the hell out of Dodge mode," running as fast as he could from the area. He wanted nothing to do with the fight; he was on probation and nowhere near the soldier that Doughboy was on the street. Vega never looked back, leaving Doughboy wounded, bleeding, and running for his life. Asshole and elbows was all Doughboy saw; Vega was gone, leaving him to live or die on his own.

After yelling out threats and challenges to the neighborhood, Arredondo put the gun back in the house, announcing, "No one had better fuck with 18th Street!" He then continued on to his sister's wedding like nothing had ever happened, feeling satisfied that he'd made his point, shooting one of the St. Pauls 13 gang bangers and sending the other running for his life. As far as he was concerned, he'd shown—for that day, anyway—that South Side 18th Street is not to be fucked with. His cousins began praising him for his shooting of the "fakers," and for the time being he was the hero.

Doughboy, meanwhile, had run down the avenue away from the gunfire and eventually got some help from an elderly Black man that saw him limping and bleeding, trying to escape from Arredondo. The man brought him into his own home, then drove him to the hospital to be treated. He didn't call for the police; calling the police in that neighborhood wasn't even considered an option.

I got the report of the shooting in the area, and when I arrived nothing was there and no one remained. No one waved me down; people just stared, watching and saying nothing. I had to walk the neighborhood and search for people willing to talk to me. Finally, I started to get witnesses talking and put together what had happened. I was there for some time, winning back the neighborhood.

I found the shoes that belonged to Doughboy, and with the witnesses' help I had a pretty good idea of what had happened—I just didn't know why. Then I got a call that a Black male had arrived at a nearby hospital, shot in the buttocks, so I headed up there to see if the call that I was on and the injured male in the hospital were related.

I met with Doughboy in the Emergency Room. I'd known him for several years already, and we had a really good relationship. He knew me from patrol, and I'd picked him up for previous gang detectives many times. I'd always treated him with respect and often took him to get a soft drink and say goodbye to his mother the times that I picked him up; this meant a lot to him and his mom.

I asked Doughboy what had happened to him, and he told me all about the incident. He told me about Vega and Arredondo and the 18th Street bangers in front of the house. He was completely straightforward about what had happened. I obtained a statement from him about what had happened, then went back to the scene. Before I left, I teased him a bit about the gunshot to the ass, and we laughed.

Usually, bangers would be proud of the scar a gunshot would produce and would show it off to their friends at parties. I joked with him that he'd be showing off his ass at SP-13 parties and that no one would wanna see it. We laughed about this for a while. then I left the Emergency Room.

I went back to the scene and talked to Arredondo's parents, who had just arrived home from the wedding and explained what had happened. The said that they didn't know where Neto was, but when he returned they'd bring him to me. They were very upset about the situation and said that he'd brought shame to the family name. To make matters worse, he'd done this at their home and on their daughter's wedding day. They were very upset by the incident.

I gave them my phone number and asked them to call when he returned, then left the residence. I returned to the station and briefed Sgt. Gus about what I'd found out, telling him that the Arredondo family said they'd call when Neto came home. He rolled his eyes and said that I was "stupid to believe a bunch of fucking Mexicans." He then said to me, "Man, where the hell have you been the last few years? Working in fucking Mayberry?"

I tried to explain to him that the Arredondo family was old school Mexico and that they had the old school Mexican values. I believed them when they said they'd be in with Neto when he came home; this was a point of honor for the entire family.

Gus shook his head and said that I "had a lot to learn about Mexicans." I was getting really pissed, so I replied, "If I'm so fucking dumb about the street, how come I've solved the past two cases you gave me with arrests—while no one else in this unit has solved shit for months?"

He got up, mumbling something about "smart ass rookie," then left the office.

I started on my case report, and a couple hours later when I was almost done, the entire Arredondo family showed up with Neto. They'd told him that he'd better confess to everything that had happened, or he'd be banished from the family and no longer considered a part of them. He did confess to everything and told me the same story that Doughboy had recounted in the Emergency Room. His father came to me afterwards and wanted to make sure that I was satisfied with the confession. He personally apologized for his son's behavior and said that he hoped that I'd call on him if I needed anything else for the case. He said that he wouldn't have his family name tarnished by this incident and that his son would make this right or be forever banished from the family. This was impressive shit to me, but not uncommon with families coming from Mexico that had the "old school" value system. That was how every old school family I ever met from Mexico was; their family name and honor was everything to them. I had tremendous respect for the Arredondos.

Neto was just a juvenile at the time, but he was eventually certified as an adult and sent to prison. When we went to court on the case, Doughboy was brought back to St. Pauls from San Marcos, where he'd returned after the shooting. He didn't know who the guy was that had shot him, but when we went to court and he saw Arredondo and heard his name, he recognized him from high school and middle school. Doughboy was shocked; he told me that he'd been friends with Arredondo in school for years.

He said, "Damn, this shit is stupid! We were friends in school. I didn't recognize him that day, and now we're in court." He was genuinely upset, but not enough to leave the gang life.

As for Neto, though, I heard through the 18th Street members that he swore off the gang life and totally left it. In letters from prison, he told them that he wouldn't be a member anymore and that he had to get his life back on track. He had to choose between his family and his gang—and he chose family. He was lucky that his family was so strict in their belief that he had to make this right.

I never saw him again, even after he got out of prison. As far as I know, that was the end of his gang affiliation.

ABOUT THE AUTHOR
ZACH FORTIER

ZACH FORTIER WAS A POLICE officer for over 30 years specializing in K-9, SWAT, gang, domestic violence, and sex crimes as an investigator. He has written three books about police work. The first book, *CurbChek,* is a case-by-case account of the streets as he worked them from the start of his career. The second book, *Street Creds*, details the time he spent in a gang task force and the cases that occurred. The third book, *Curbchek-Reload,* is by far the most gritty. The author is dangerously damaged, suffering from post-traumatic stress syndrome (PTSD) and the day-to-day violence of working the street. *Hero To Zero,* his fourth book, details the incredibly talented cops that he worked with but ended up going down in flames. Some ended up in prison and one on the FBI's ten most wanted list.

If you are looking for gritty, true crime stories, be sure to check out all of Zach Fortier's novels.